W9-BAQ-725

BASKETBALL

Fifth Edition

About the Author

Head basketball coach at Stetson University since 1957, Glenn Wilkes has compiled an enviable record there of 480 wins and 359 losses, and an outstanding overall coaching record of 603–389. Among collegiate coaches, he ranks in the top ten in number of wins.

Through his writing and public speaking, Wilkes has imparted his knowledge of basketball to a wide audience. He has written numerous articles on basketball and authored four other books: *Winning Basketball Strategy* (1959), *Basketball Coach's Complete Handbook* (1962), *Fundamentals of Coaching Basketball* (1982), and *Basketball's Three-Point Shot* (1987). He has lectured at numerous clinics throughout the nation and in Europe and South America. He also directs basketball schools for boys and girls and founded one of the most successful coaching clinics in the nation.

Wilkes earned his A.B. at Mercer University and his M.A. and Ed.D. degrees at George Peabody College.

BASKETBALL
Fifth Edition

Glenn Wilkes
Stetson University

Wm. C. Brown Publishers

Book Team

Editor *Chris Rogers*
Developmental Editor *Cindy Kuhrasch*
Production Coordinator *Carla D. Arnold*

 Wm. C. Brown Publishers

President *G. Franklin Lewis*
Vice President, Editor-in-Chief *George Wm. Bergquist*
Vice President, Director of Production *Beverly Kolz*
Vice President, National Sales Manager *Bob McLaughlin*
Director of Marketing *Thomas E. Doran*
Marketing Communications Manager *Edward Bartell*
Marketing Manager *Kathy Law Laube*
Production Editorial Manager *Colleen A. Yonda*
Production Editorial Manager *Julie A. Kennedy*
Publishing Services Manager *Karen J. Slaght*
Manager of Visuals and Design *Faye M. Schilling*

Wm. C. Brown Sports and Fitness Series
Consulting Editor
Physical Education
Aileene Lockhart
Texas Women's University

Sports and Fitness Series
Evaluation Materials Editor
Jane A. Mott
Texas Women's University

Cover photo by Bob Coyle

Cover design by Jeanne Marie Regan

Library of Congress Catalog Card Number: 88–63889

ISBN 0–697–07273–8

Printed in the United States of America by Wm. C. Brown Publishers,
2460 Kerper Boulevard, Dubuque, IA 52001

10 9 8 7 6 5 4 3 2 1

Contents

Preface   ix
Key to Diagrams   xi

The Game of Basketball   1

1

Skills Essential for Every Player   3

2

Holding the Basketball	3
Shooting the Basketball	4
Secret to Good Shooting, Basic Types of Shots, Shooting Essentials	
Passing and Receiving the Ball	13
Types of Passes, Passing Hints	
Dribbling	18
Dribbling Hints	
Pivoting	20
Rebounding	20
Defensive Rebounding, Offensive Rebounding	
Individual Defense	22
Defensive Hints	

Better Players Master These Techniques   29

3

Shooting	29
Passing	30
Dribbling	31
Dribble Drills	
The One-on-One Offensive Situation	35

Progress Can Be Speeded Up **39**

4

Seek Professional Help and Advice 39

Practice with a Purpose 39

Shooting, Dribbling, Passing, Rebounding, Footwork, Individual Defense

Take Advantage of Every Opportunity to Play 42

Watch Games and Films 42

Keep in Good Physical Condition 43

Get a Proper Warm-Up Before Practice 44

Take Care of Your Feet 44

Offensive Patterns of Play **45**

5

Major Essentials for a Sound Team Offense 45

Offensive Patterns Against the Man-for-Man Defense 47

Zone Offense 54

The Fast Break 57

When to Fast-Break

Out-of-Bounds Situations 59

The Three-Point Shot 60

The Argument Over Distance, Advantages of the Three-Point Shot, Disadvantages of the Three-Point Shot, Techniques for Getting the Three-Point Shot, Special Three-Point Plays

Defensive Patterns of Play **63**

6

Team Defensive Essentials 63

Man-for-Man Defense 65

General Principles for Man-for-Man Team Defense

Defensive Positioning 66

Zone Defense 68

Advantages of Zone Defense 69

Disadvantages of Zone Defense, General Principles for Zone Defense, Types of Zone Defenses, Pressing Zone Defenses

Combination Defenses 73

One Defense or Several?

The Strategy of the Game **75**

7

Individual Strategy 75

Team Strategy 75

Playing for One, When to Press, When to Freeze, The Use of Time-Outs, Strategy for the Three-Point Shot

Origin and Development of Basketball   83

8

Significant Rule Changes	83
The Most Significant Rule Change for Women, The Three-Point Shot	
The Jump Shot	85
"Dunking"	85
Gymnasium Development	85
The Four Most Famous Teams	86
Language of the Game	86

Rules of the Game   91

9

Playing Court, Goal, and Ball	91
Players and Substitutes	91
Scoring and Timing	92
Specific Rule Definitions	93
Violations and Penalties	94

Sportsmanship in Basketball   97

10

Facts for Enthusiasts   99

11

Playing the Game   101

12

Questions and Answers   103
Index   111

Preface

Basketball is a thrilling game, exciting for both the participant and the spectator. Because the equipment is inexpensive and the game so popular, opportunities to play or watch basketball are very numerous.

Information applicable to both the beginner and the more advanced player and for both men and women is given in the following pages. The fundamentals are explained and illustrated. Mastery of these fundamentals is absolutely necessary, for they are basic to any level of play—good body mechanics, good ball handling, and excellent footwork are prerequisites to more advanced play. In addition, strategy and team tactics for both the offense and defense are emphasized. The player should always remember that basketball is a *team* game and that the *individual* succeeds only as much as the *team* succeeds.

Self-evaluation questions throughout the book afford typical examples of the kinds of understanding and levels of skill that the reader should be attempting to acquire. The learner should consider these as examples and pose additional ones as a self-check on progress. Since the order in which the text is read and the progression used by the teacher or coach are matters of individual decision, the evaluative materials are not always positioned according to the presentation of given topics. In some instances the reader may find it difficult to respond fully to a question until all the material has been studied or more playing experience acquired. Thus, the reader should return to troublesome questions or physical challenges from time to time until being sure of the answers or developing the skills called for, as the case may be.

Key to Diagrams

Defensive Player	X
Offensive Player with Ball	O•
Offensive Player without Ball	O
Path of Player	→
Screen	—⊢
Pass	------→
Dribble	∼∼∼→

The Game of Basketball

1

Basketball is a team sport played by millions the world over, and its popularity seems to increase constantly. It is one of the world's fastest sports, and accomplished play requires speed, stamina, and a high degree of skill. It can be enjoyed on an amateur basis, however, in which case intensive training or previous experience is not required.

College teams play the game on a court ninety-four feet long by fifty feet wide. An eighteen-inch cylinder called the *basket* or goal is attached to a backboard four feet high by six feet wide at each end of the court. The objective of each team is to score by causing the ball to go through the basket that is defended by its opponents. A successful shot during regular play is called a field goal and scores either two or three points depending on the distance away from the basket from which it is made. An unguarded shot from the free throw line, awarded for fouls made by the opponents, is called a free throw or foul shot, and counts one point. There is no other method of scoring.

Since the only way to score is by shooting the ball through the opponent's basket, considerable emphasis is placed on the development of shooting skills. A variety of shots is used and these are discussed in succeeding chapters of this book.

The ball may be advanced from one end of the court to the other either by passing or dribbling. Passing the ball is throwing it from one player to another. Dribbling the ball is bouncing it on the court in a way that will enable the player to advance it. More emphasis is placed on passing than on dribbling because the ball can be advanced quicker by this means; in addition, clever passing enhances teamwork and makes a team more difficult to defend against. John Wooden, who coached UCLA to ten national championships, considers passing to be the most important of individual offensive fundamentals.[1]

A team is comprised of five players. When on offense a team uses a variety of plays or maneuvers that are designed to gain a clear shot at the basket. Once a shot is taken, the offensive team attempts to have several of its taller players in position to rebound any missed shot.

When a team is on defense, its members may use a variety of defenses to prevent its opponents from getting an open shot at the basket. They may play man-for-man defense, in which each player goes with an assigned opponent wherever that opponent goes, or they may play a zone defense, in which each member of the team is assigned a particular area of the floor to defend. A combination of man-for-man and zone defenses may be used. In addition, a team may guard its opponents all over the court or fall back near the basket it is defending. No matter what type of defense is used, when the opponent does shoot, the object of the defense is to rebound any missed shot in order to keep the opponent from obtaining possession of the ball and thus getting additional scoring opportunities.

Since both the offensive and defensive teams are fighting for possession of the ball after missed shots, it follows that a primary method of obtaining the ball is by rebounding. Most coaches feel that the team which "controls the boards" will win the majority of the time. Considerable attention therefore is placed on rebounding, both offensively and defensively, and tall players as well as those with excellent jumping ability are sought as players.

The game is played rapidly, and the ball usually changes hands every fifteen or twenty seconds as the result of a score, a rebound, a bad pass, or a violation. Modern basketball shooters have become quite proficient and team shooting percentages are increasing constantly. This has resulted in high-scoring games at virtually all levels of play.

The frequency of scoring, the fast-moving pace, and rules that are easily understood have combined to make basketball one of the most popular spectator sports. Top college and professional teams regularly play before crowds of 10,000, and some of the larger college arenas seat as many as 18,000 or more. The University of Tennessee opened a new arena in 1987 that seats 25,000, while the University of Kentucky's Rupp Arena has a seating capacity of 23,000 and is sold out for every game. It is not uncommon for high-school gymnasiums to have provisions for several thousand spectators.

What is the game of basketball really like? It's fast, exciting, fun to play, and enjoyable to watch. In the pages that follow, a more detailed description of the game will be given so you can play the game for fun and watch it with maximum enjoyment.

Note

1. John R. Wooden, *Practical Modern Basketball*, 3rd ed. (New York: Macmillan Publishing Company, 1988), 83.

Skills Essential for Every Player

2

There are specific skills that must be learned if you are to participate in basketball. How proficient you must be varies with the level of play. All players, however, must be able to perform certain basic shots, pass and receive the ball, dribble, pivot, rebound to a certain extent, and have a fundamental understanding of defensive skills.

Since a basketball team is made up of participants playing several positions, the degree to which each specific skill must be developed varies with each position. A guard will have to excell in ball handling and dribbling more than in rebounding. A forward or center will not be required to handle the ball as much as a guard, but must shoulder much more of the rebounding responsibilities.

Holding the Basketball

Before the ball can be shot, passed, or dribbled, it is important to know how to hold it. Holding it improperly will result in faulty execution of other fundamentals.

The most important thing to remember is that *the palms of the hands should never touch the ball*. The ball should be held in the fingers, with the fingers spread comfortably but as widely as possible (fig. 2.1). The ball is held in this manner whether one is shooting or passing.

When a player receives the ball in scoring position in the front court, the ball normally should be held close to the hip on the side of the shooting hand. This enables the player to shoot, drive, or pass and is commonly termed the *triple-threat position*.

Figure 2.1
Holding the ball.

Shooting the Basketball

Shooting is one of the most important fundamentals in the game of basketball. Without good shooters, a team may possess brilliant passers, superb dribblers, excellent rebounders, and other strong assets, but still may find it difficult to win consistently. Many coaches feel that shooters are born and not made, and the brilliant play of some of the nation's great shooters today lends support to this argument. Surely some players do possess the "touch" that other players strive a lifetime to achieve. However, the vast majority of good shooters are "made" shooters who have combined sound shooting fundamentals with countless hours of practice to develop themselves into good percentage shooters.

Secret to Good Shooting

Is there a secret to good shooting? If such a secret exists, it is this: countless hours of *practice, practice,* and *more practice!* Why do all coaches love to see goals nailed to the sides of garages in students' backyards? Simply because these goals afford opportunities for hours and hours of shooting practice by prospective basketball players. Probably more shooters have been made in backyard practice than ever have been made in gymnasiums.

Basic Types of Shots

There are three basic shots that all players should learn:

1. The lay-up shot
2. The jump shot
3. The free throw or foul shot

The Lay-Up Shot

The basic shot is the lay-up shot, which is taken close to the basket at the end of a drive or after receiving a pass from a teammate. Since it is taken from such close range, a high degree of accuracy should be expected.

As you catch the ball, either from a pass or from your dribble, your right foot should be in contact with the floor (assuming you are to shoot right-handed). Carry the ball with both hands to a position outside your right hip and step onto your left foot. As you leap into the air off your left foot, bring the ball to a position above your head and push it to the basket with your right hand. Your target should be a spot on the backboard twelve to fifteen inches above the goal. The ball should strike this spot and drop softly down through the goal. A common error many players make in shooting the lay-up is failure to shoot the ball high enough on the board. So make certain you shoot at a target some twelve to fifteen inches above the goal.

If you are a beginner and are just learning to shoot the lay-up shot, it will be best to practice it without using a dribble. Stand on both feet about two steps away from the goal. Step onto your left foot, spring into the air, and take the shot. As you begin to become somewhat proficient at making the shot after one

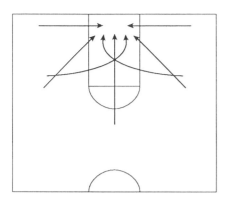

Figure 2.2
The lay-up shot should be practiced from various angles on both the right and left sides of the basket, and down the middle of the court.

step, move back to a position about even with the free-throw line. Now take three steps without using a dribble. First step onto your left foot, then your right, then your left, and take the shot. As this footwork becomes comfortable to you, add one dribble, using the same footwork.

You must be able to make the lay-up shot while driving to the basket from different angles; therefore, practice the lay-up shot from both the right and left sides of the basket, along either baseline, while driving down the middle, and from other angles where you may be able to obtain a lay-up opportunity (fig. 2.2).

Practice the shot with both the right hand and the left hand so you will be able to shoot with either, depending upon which side of the basket you are driving from. This will, of course, require you to be able to use either foot for the takeoff.

Avoid developing the habit of "broad-jumping" the lay-up shot. This common error is caused by failure to spring upward as the shot is taken, a move that is needed to brake the forward momentum caused by the drive to the basket. Failure to jump upward decreases the accuracy of the shot because (1) you are not as close to the basket as you could be, and (2) the forward momentum of the body causes the ball to be released harder against the backboard. In addition, the forward momentum of the body often will cause you to charge into an opponent, resulting in an offensive foul. Therefore, as you practice the lay-up shot, make certain that the spring from your takeoff foot is upward rather than forward (fig. 2.3).

Place a strip of masking tape on the backboard twelve inches above the basket. Can you aim ten lay-up shots from alternate sides of the goal so that each one strikes the backboard above the tape line?

In addition to broad-jumping the lay-up, other common beginners' errors that you must strive to avoid are

1. *Jumping off the wrong foot.* If you are shooting with your right hand, it is important to jump or "take off" from the left foot. The opposite is true when shooting with the left hand. Shooting off the correct foot is one of the most difficult fundamentals for the beginning player to master when learning to shoot the lay-up.

Figure 2.3
The lay-up shot in a game situation.
Courtesy Stetson University Sports
Information.

2. *Laying the ball against the board too hard.* The softer you can lay the ball against the backboard the better your chances of making the shot.
3. *Putting spin or "English" on the ball.* Any spin on the ball should be that caused by the natural release of the ball and not because of any conscious effort to cause spin.
4. *Shooting the ball too low on the backboard.* This is one of the more common errors even of accomplished players. They will shoot the ball at a spot no higher than six to eight inches above the goal instead of the more desirable twelve to fifteen inches.
5. *Holding the ball too loosely on the takeoff.* Many players hold the ball so loosely on the takeoff that they will miss any shot attempt should contact from the defense occur. If the ball is held firmly, contact can be made by an opponent and the shot still can be made. This will result in what is commonly called the "three-point play"—making the basket and the resulting one free throw awarded for the foul.
6. *Failure to concentrate.* The shot is so easy that players have a tendency to take the shot for granted and lose their concentration on the shot. Concentration is important in order to avoid some of the common errors mentioned above.

The Jump Shot

Though the jump shot did not become popular until the 1950s, it is now the most popular and effective shot in basketball. Modern jump shooters have become extremely proficient from as far as twenty-five feet from the basket. Because the shot is taken after the shooter has jumped into the air, it is very difficult to defense. This has resulted in a greater improvement in scoring than any other basketball innovation.

Prior to jumping into the air for the shot, hold the ball in both hands with your shoulders square to the goal and your knees slightly bent. The right-handed shooter should have the right foot slightly forward of the left foot, with both feet pointing toward the basket. The jump into the air is made with an upward thrust by both legs. Height of the jump will vary with the individual but, as a general rule, do not leap as high as possible but take a smooth, effortless jump into the air for the shot. As the jump is made the ball is brought to a position slightly above and in front of your head. Your left hand should be on the side of the ball for control and the back of your right hand should be facing you. It is very important that your right elbow be under the ball and on a line between you and the basket. Sight at the goal just under the ball. The shot is released by an upward movement of your right elbow and a simultaneous forward push of your forearm and wrist. The ball should leave from the index and middle fingers of the right hand. Your wrist should snap completely forward to provide a good follow-through (figs. 2.4–2.9).

Balance is very important to the success of the shot. Many shooters fall forward, sideways, or backwards when taking the jump shot; this decreases accuracy and often leads to offensive fouls. You should initiate the shot from a balanced position and jump *straight upwards.*

Practice the jump shot from three situations: (1) from a stationary position, (2) after a dribble, and (3) after cutting to receive a pass. Balance and the upward jump are more difficult in the latter two situations but are of no less importance.

Why is it so important to jump vertically when you do a lay-up shot? When you do a jump shot?

Jump-Shooting Hints

1. *Always practice shots you will shoot in a game.* If you play center or forward, it is foolish to spend a great deal of time practicing shots from the guard position, for example.
2. Practice shooting *under game conditions if possible.* If you can find an opponent to challenge, the competition will be beneficial. If you are shooting alone, use your imagination to dream up games that will challenge you to do your best and involve earning a score.
3. *Never force the shot.* If you are closely guarded, pass to someone else or make a maneuver to get open for the shot.
4. *Learn to relax when shooting.* The more practice you get under competitive situations, the easier it will be for you to relax when shooting.

Figure 2.4
The jump shot. Notice the position of the right elbow and the intense concentration of the eyes on the basket.

Figure 2.5
The jump shot just before release of the ball.

Figure 2.6
The jump shot just after release of the ball. Notice the follow-through wrist action of the shooting hand, and that the eyes are still concentrating on the target.

Figure 2.7
The jump shot in a game situation.

Figure 2.8
Another view of the jump shot in actual play. Notice that the shooting arm is fully extended on the follow-through. Courtesy Stetson University Sports Information.

Figure 2.9
The jump shooter has just released his left hand from the ball and is beginning his follow-through motion.

5. *Never attempt wild or crazy shots.*
6. *Always follow through.*
7. *Do not shoot when a teammate is in a better position to shoot.*

Competition makes goal-shooting practice more realistic and interesting. Can you devise a game for each of these situations: one player, partners, three or four players?

Common Errors in Shooting the Jump Shot

1. *Shooting while off balance.*
2. *Improper elbow position.* Many poor jump-shooters have their elbow too far away from the body when shooting. Many shooters hold the elbow too high, which forces the ball on top or behind the head resulting in a line-drive type of shot rather than a soft, arching shot.
3. *Poor target area.* It is important that the shooter concentrate on a specific area of the basket at which to shoot. Some players aim at the front of the rim, others at the back of the rim, while others aim at the middle of the basket. Any can be correct as long as the player consistently aims at the same target and knows exactly what that target is.
4. *Faulty foot position.* The shot actually begins with the feet. Having the feet too wide apart or the toes pointing sideways will result in poor body balance and lower accuracy.
5. *Forcing the shot.* Since the jump shot is taken from the height of the jump, many players feel they can shoot it even though they are closely guarded. This forcing of the shot results in decreased accuracy and is very bad for team morale.

What Is A Good Shot?

First, *you must have the ability to shoot the shot.* What may be a good shot for one player may be a bad shot for another. The twenty-foot jump shot by a guard could be a percentage shot, whereas the same shot taken by a big center could very well be a bad shot. Players must shoot within their range.

Second, *you must not be closely guarded.* An exception is when you are close to the basket and can make a power move.

Third, *rebounders must be in position to rebound any missed shot.* Few things are more irritating in basketball than the player "gunning the ball up" from twenty feet out with no one near the rebounding area.

Shooting Games

There are a number of games or contests you can play with a teammate that will add competition and interest to shooting practice. Among these games are:

1. *Twenty-One.* Start at a spot approximately twenty feet from the basket. Shoot a long jump shot, then retrieve the ball and shoot a lay-up. The long shot counts two points, the lay-up shot counts one point. If both shots are made, continue shooting. The first player to reach a total of twenty-one points is the winner. Variety can be added by not allowing a short shot until a long shot is made and by requiring that the player's last shot be a long shot.
2. *Basketball Golf.* Draw nine circles in various locations around the court. Attempt to make a shot from each circle, shooting only one shot from each. Your score is the number of shots made.

3. *Riskit.* This game is similar to basketball golf. If you miss a shot, you can have a second chance. However, if you miss the second shot, you must return to the starting point. The first player making a shot at all nine circles is the winner.

4. *Horse.* This is one of the most popular playground games. One player selects a type and location for a shot and shoots. If the shot is made, the opponent must duplicate the shot. If the shot is missed, the opponent may select a different type and location for a shot. Any missed shot after a made shot results in the player missing the shot getting the letter H. Subsequent misses get other letters of the word horse. The object of the game is to make your opponent spell out the five letters of the word before you do.

The Free Throw or Foul Shot

Because every participant will be fouled at one time or another, it is necessary for all players to be able to shoot free throws or foul shots. A team may be big and talented but a bad shooting night at the free throw line will result in defeat.

Many years ago the majority of shooters used a two-handed underhand method to shoot free throws; in fact, Bunny Leavitt used that method to set a world record when he scored 499 consecutive free throws. Rick Barry became one of the leading free throw shooters in the NBA using the underhand method. However, the popularity of that method has declined and virtually all players today use a one-handed push-shot method for shooting free throws. This is because the same basic shot used in regular play also can be used from the free throw line, and the additional practice that would be required to develop the underhand method is not necessary.

Free Throw Shooting Technique

For a one-hand free throw, the right-handed shooter stands with the right foot approximately one inch behind the free throw line with the left foot approximately twelve inches back. The feet should be shoulder-width apart and the knees slightly bent. Balance must be maintained, though most of the weight will be forward. The ball is held by both hands and just in front of the face. As when shooting the jump shot, your left hand should be on the side of the ball in order to control it, and the back of your right hand should be facing you. Elbows should be comfortably close to your body. The shot is initiated by a simultaneous straightening of your knees and raising of your right elbow. As the elbow is raised, a forward push of your forearm and snap of your wrist pushes the ball toward the basket. The ball should leave from the index and middle finger of your right hand. Complete follow-through should leave your right arm fully extended and your right wrist broken completely over so that your palm faces downward.

Proper shooting mechanics are a necessity for good free throw shooting. However, three additional factors determine just how successful a player will become at the free throw line.

1. *Relaxation.* You cannot shoot well if you are tense. Therefore, you must acquire the ability to relax when you are at the free throw line. Most players develop a routine they go through to help them relax prior to shooting. Examples of routines for relaxation are taking three or four deep breaths before shooting, or bouncing the ball several times before shooting.
2. *Concentration.* You must develop the ability to concentrate solely on the free throw shot. You cannot be thinking of some distracting action possibly being made by an opponent, or of the actions of the spectators, or of a photographer who may be taking a picture.
3. *Practice.* Virtually all players can learn to shoot free throws well if they are willing to practice enough. Practice under competitive situations whenever possible. Challenge teammates to free throw shooting contests often. Competitive practice aids concentration and will result in improved shooting in an actual game.

Free Throw Drills You Can Do Alone or with a Partner

1. See how many free throws you can make without missing. Set your own goal. Attempt to make ten in a row, then twenty-five in a row. Compete against your partner.
2. Shoot a designated number of free throws. Run a wind sprint or do push-ups for each miss. This will help your shooting concentration and also help keep you in good physical condition.
3. Ten-Point Game. Start with ten points. Shoot free throws. A miss adds a point to your total while a made free throw subtracts a point. The object is to get to zero.

By practicing free throws you may improve your jump shot and vice versa. What are the elements of technique common to both?

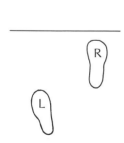

Figure 2.10
Ordinary free-throw stance for a right-handed player.

PROPER SHOOTING FORM
= HOURS OF PRACTICE
+ CONFIDENCE
= A GOOD SHOOTER!

Figure 2.11
The chart shows the three key ingredients necessary to become a good shooter.

Shooting Essentials

Varying techniques are used when shooting each type of shot. However, several essentials for all types of shots are listed below.

1. *Good Vision.* Players must be able to see the goal clearly if they are to develop the consistent depth perception that will enable them to shoot a good percentage. Players who wear glasses all day and then remove them for the basketball game that night cannot expect to be good shooters. Contact lens or glass guards may be bothersome but may prove necessary to assure good shooting ability.
2. *Good Hand Position.* The ball should be held with fingers spread widely and with the *palms off the ball.*
3. *Concentration.* When aiming for the basket, the shooter must be concentrating on the shot with the eyes centered on the target.
4. *Relaxation.* Muscles must be functioning properly during the shooting motion. Tenseness will prevent this.
5. *Follow-through.* The shooter must follow through on all types of shots. This is a common error committed by many shooters and its correction often improves shooting percentage tremendously.
6. *Confidence.* Shooters must believe that they are going to make the shot. Ask the great shooters and they will tell you that they never take a shot that they don't think they're going to make! If the shooter is merely putting the ball in the air and hoping it will go in the basket, both the shooter and the team would be far better off if a pass was made to someone else for the shot attempt.

Passing and Receiving the Ball

Passing and receiving the basketball are skills as important as shooting. By clever passes, the ball can be advanced into the area of the court where high percentage shots can be obtained; but the most clever pass can be completely ineffectual if the receiver cannot catch the ball and a fumble results.

If the ball is to be properly received, the hands should be cupped so the heels of the hands are three or four inches apart, with fingers spread comfortably and thumbs almost parallel. The arms should be extended. As the ball strikes the hands, you should "give" with the pass—in other words, flex the elbows in such a manner that your hands move in toward your body as the ball is received. This is tremendously important, for stiff arms and hands result in many fumbled passes. To emphasize this point, think of throwing a basketball against a brick wall. What will it do? Rebound back to the passer, of course! Now think of throwing a basketball against a blanket hung over a clothesline. What will happen to the basketball? The blanket will give, and the ball will drop to the ground instead of rebounding to the passer. This is the type of softness pass receivers must have for proper ball handling.

To be a good pass receiver you must learn to "look the ball into your hands." In other words, you must keep your eyes on the pass until it strikes your hands. Failure to maintain this necessary hand-eye coordination is a major cause of fumbled passes. Players actually start to dribble or pass before the ball gets to them.

Another cause of poor receiving is a lack of concentration. Players often take the pass for granted, assuming it can be caught easily. The assumption would be correct if you did not have to contend with interference from the defense.

Receiving is a fundamental skill just as important as passing. One is dependent on the other. You must place a great deal of emphasis on learning to make good passes, but you must place just as much emphasis on learning to receive the ball properly.

Under actual game conditions it is not unusual for a receiver to fail to catch an easy pass. What can you do to avoid this error?

Types of Passes

Four types of passes are essential for all players:

1. Chest pass
2. Bounce pass
3. Flip pass
4. Two-hand overhead pass

Figure 2.12
A player in passing position.

Chest Pass

The most common pass in basketball is the chest pass. In fact, when we think of passing as a part of basketball we immediately think of this type of pass. The ball is held in both hands with the fingers comfortably spread. *Remember, the palms of the hands do not touch the ball.* Your thumbs point at an angle to each other. The ball is directly in front of your chest. The pass is made with a forward thrust of your arms and a simultaneous snap of your wrists. Complete arm extension is necessary for proper follow-through. The palms of your hands should be downward at the completion of the pass. It is important that the pass be thrown so the receiver can receive it about the waist but not above the head.

Bounce Pass

The bounce pass is made in the same manner as the chest pass; however, it is pushed down to the floor and bounces up to the pass receiver. This is a good pass to use in order to pass by a taller opponent or feed a teammate who is in close to the basket. Considerable practice is necessary to enable you to know how far from the receiver the ball should strike the floor. If it strikes the floor too far away from the receiver, the ball will float into the air and be easily intercepted. On the other hand, if the ball strikes the floor too close to the receiver, it will be difficult for the receiver to handle the pass (fig. 2.13).

Flip Pass

The flip pass is necessary during a close exchange of the ball, as, for example, on a close weave when the ball is "flipped" softly from one player to another. The pass is made by placing the passing hand directly under the ball and flipping the wrist so the ball will flip into the air. The ball should be flipped softly *upward,* not outward, and should not be flipped more than a few inches above your hand. This type of pass is easily received by a player cutting to the basket. It is used by post players in feeding cutters, and the dribbling screener uses it to pass to players cutting by the screen.

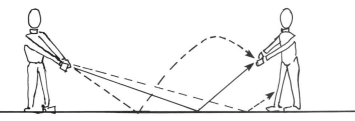

Figure 2.13
The solid line represents the correct path of the bounce pass, while the broken lines indicate incorrect paths. The bounce pass that strikes the floor too close to the receiver usually bounces too low for easy handling, while the bounce pass that strikes the floor too far away from the receiver bounces too high in the air and is easily intercepted.

With masking tape, outline a two-foot square on a smooth wall and then surround it with a three-foot square. Standing fifteen feet back, practice ten chest passes and ten bounce passes to the target, counting two points for hits in the inner square and one point for hits in the outer. What is your score for each type of pass?

Two-Hand Overhead Pass

The two-hand overhead pass is very effective for passing the ball over the head of a defensive player and into a teammate in the pivot area. The ball is held in both hands with arms almost fully extended over the head. The heel of each hand faces toward the target. Make the pass by thrusting both arms forward and snapping both wrists in order to impart speed to the pass. At the completion of the pass, your fingers should face the target (figs. 2.14, 2.15).

Passing Hints

1. Don't "telegraph" the pass. Look one way and pass another.
2. Fake the chest pass and throw the bounce pass. Fake the bounce pass and throw the chest pass.
3. Follow through.
4. Keep the palms off the ball.
5. Throw the flip pass in close quarters (fig. 2.16).
6. Pass to the receiver on the side away from the defensive player.
7. Pass to the region of the receiver's chest. Passes are more easily handled there, and the receiver is in position to make another pass without adjusting to the height of the ball.

Figure 2.14
The two-hand overhead pass. Courtesy Stetson University Sports Information.

Figure 2.15
The two-hand overhead pass in actual play.

Figure 2.16
The flip pass.

Dribbling

The dribble is used to advance the ball downcourt, to initiate play patterns, to make drives to the basket, and to move into good shooting position when pass receivers are closely guarded.

Place five or six chairs in a straight line about five feet apart. Dribble in and out of the chairs using the right hand when on the right side of the chair and the left hand when on the left. Keep the head and eyes straight ahead and do not look down at the ball. Can you make two complete circuits without a miss? In how many seconds can you make the two circuits?

The dribble technique is relatively simple and can be mastered easily with proper practice. The dribble is executed by pushing the ball to the floor with a snap of your wrist and downward motion of your forearm. Fingers should be comfortably spread in order to achieve maximum control of the dribble. It is important that you learn to dribble (a) *without looking at the ball,* and (b) *with either hand.* Dribbling without looking at the ball enables you to see teammates who might break into the clear. The ability to dribble with either hand is necessary so you can drive in any direction, therefore making the defensive players' task more difficult.

It is also necessary to learn both (1) the speed dribble, and (2) the control dribble. The speed dribble is used when you must advance the ball quickly downcourt and no defensive players are harassing you. Your body should be in an upright position and the ball is pushed out in front of you. When defensive players are near and the ball must be protected, use the control dribble. In this case your knees should be bent so that your body will be low and the ball is dribbled lower and closer to the body (fig. 2.17).

Figure 2.17
Dribbling position. Knees bent. Head up. Eyes ahead.

It is almost as important for you to learn *when* to dribble as *how* to dribble. The dribble often is misused, and it is detrimental to the morale of the team when a player monopolizes the ball by over-dribbling. Though no iron-clad rule can be made indicating when to dribble, a general guide is to *avoid dribbling when it is more advantageous to pass.* Remember that the ball can be moved much more quickly by passing than by dribbling, and that quick movement of the ball makes a team very difficult to guard.

As you are moving down the court with the ball in your possession, a defensive player closes in from your right side. Which type of dribble would you use and with which hand? What should you do if defensive players are closing in from both sides?

Dribbling Hints

1. If a pass is more advantageous to your team, do not dribble.
2. Do not look at the ball when dribbling.
3. Learn to dribble equally well with either hand.
4. Do not develop the habit of taking a dribble immediately upon receiving a pass. Save your dribble as a threat to your opponent.
5. Do not "bat" the ball. Push it to the floor.
6. Never attempt to dribble between two defensive players.
7. Remember—it is as important to know *when* to dribble as *how* to dribble.

Figure 2.18
The dribble in a game situation.

Figure 2.19
Using the body to protect the ball when the dribbler is closely guarded. Notice that the dribbler has his head up and is looking for open teammates. Courtesy Stetson University Sports Information.

Figure 2.20
The simple pivot. The dark area represents the position of the offensive player's feet at the end of the dribble, while the dotted lines indicate foot position after pivoting away from defensive player X to protect the ball.

Pivoting

Proper pivoting techniques must be mastered by all players in order to prevent "traveling" or "walking" violations. The rules of the game allow the player holding the ball to step in any direction with one foot while keeping the other foot, called the *pivot* foot, at its point of contact with the floor. The player may continue to move the other foot as long as the ball of the pivot foot remains in position. The primary purpose of the pivot is to enable the ball handler to pivot the body between an opponent and the basket to protect the ball. Once the pivot foot has been established, it cannot be changed without involving an intervening dribble or pass.

The *simple pivot* is normally used at the end of a dribble or after receiving a pass and is the only pivoting technique the beginning player needs to master. The dribble or pass is received into both hands with one foot in advance of the other. Your rear foot becomes the pivot. You can move your front foot in any direction as long as the ball of your rear foot remains in contact with the floor (fig. 2.20). It is very important that the pivot be made on the ball of your foot; a pivot on your heel results in a violation.

Rebounding

Rebounding missed shot attempts is one of the most important facets of the game. The team that controls the majority of the rebounds usually wins despite weaknesses in other areas of play. It is because good rebounding is so necessary that the tall player has become so important to the game. Though the position a player plays will determine how often the player is in position to rebound, all players must learn proper rebounding techniques. Throughout the game all players will have an opportunity to rebound either offensively or defensively, and usually both.

Defensive Rebounding

When an opponent shoots, defensive players must prepare immediately for the defensive rebound. They cannot wait until it is determined whether the shot is missed. They must immediately position their bodies between their respective opponents and the basket to prevent an offensive rebound and the resultant second shot attempt. This maneuver—keeping the body between the opponent and the basket—is referred to as "blocking" or "screening" off the boards, or a "block-out."

As the shot is taken, step into the path of your opponent, pivot your body so your back is against your opponent, and use a slide step to keep between the opponent and the basket. Your eyes must be on the ball; therefore, you must "feel" your opponent with your rear and back. Your elbows should be out, your hands up, and your knees flexed, ready to spring. As the ball starts coming downward, jump into the air as high as possible, keeping your body spread in order to take up as much room as possible. Grab the ball tightly with both hands and land on the floor on the balls of your feet. You must keep the ball moving to keep your opponent from obtaining joint possession of it and getting a jump ball. Be careful not to sling your elbows back and forth in your efforts to protect the ball. Though this affords good ball protection, the method became so popular several seasons ago that there was considerable danger of bodily injury. Thus the rules were amended, making it a violation to sling elbows in this manner. You can keep the ball moving without slinging your elbows, and this ball movement is very important for protecting possession.

Figure 2.21
Defensive rebounding in actual game play.

Offensive Rebounding

The offensive player must go for the rebound the instant a shot is taken. In fact, the great offensive rebounders *anticipate* a shot attempt and *move into rebounding position before the shot is taken.* Larry Bird of the Boston Celtics is probably the best example of this offensive rebounding technique. It is amazing how many offensive rebounds Bird gets in a game simply by anticipating a shot by a teammate and moving into rebounding position before the defense makes a move. When this is done, it is difficult for the defense to use block-out tactics to prevent the offensive rebound.

Since the objective of the defensive rebounder is to block or screen the offensive opponent off the board, the offensive player therefore must attempt to counteract this defensive objective. Since the defensive player must feel the offensive player in order to have continuous success at blocking off, the offensive player must prevent this by moving away from the defensive player, even if it means stepping away from the basket. Once no contact exists between the offense and defense, the offense can move toward the basket with less interference. Faking in one direction and cutting in another is very difficult for the defense to handle. Clever fakes and changes of direction are essential ingredients of the successful offensive rebounder.

What the offensive rebounder does after a successful rebound is determined a great deal by how far from the basket the rebound is obtained. Since most offensive rebounds are obtained near the basket in a high-percentage shooting area and at a time when it is difficult for the defense to adjust, the rebounder should shoot the ball immediately in the majority of cases. However, the rebounder should expect contact on the shot and thus power the ball at the basket in such a manner as to be able to score despite the contact. In the case of obtaining a long offensive rebound, the rebounder may or may not elect to shoot dependent on the situation. A teammate may be more open near the basket for a pass, or the rebounder may elect to take the ball out and set up a play.

Individual Defense

As in all team sports, a strong team defense is required for successful play. Though a variety of team defenses may be used, strength will depend a great deal on the specific defensive skills of the individual members of the team. This individual defensive ability depends upon six major factors:

1. Desire
2. Stance
3. Footwork
4. Position
5. Vision
6. Defensive talk

Desire

Players tend not to enjoy playing defense as much as they enjoy playing offense. Therefore, they tend to loaf on defense, anxiously waiting for their team to get the ball. If you want to be a good defensive player, you must *want* to play defense. You must take pride in your efforts to defend an opponent and look forward to defensive opportunities. Develop a genuine desire to play defense and you will be surprised at what you can achieve on the defensive end of the court.

Stance

Individual defensive play demands quick movement to counteract offensive maneuvers. This quick movement is almost impossible unless you maintain the correct defensive stance. Assume a position with one foot in advance of the other and your knees bent so that your rear will be low. Your back should be straight and your head up to permit good vision (fig. 2.22). The position of your hands will depend on whether you are guarding a player with or without the ball, and whether or not a player with the ball is dribbling or holding the ball in a shooting or passing position. When guarding a player without the ball, one hand should be down, with the other hand in the passing lane to discourage your opponent from receiving a pass. When guarding a player in a shooting or passing position, the hand on the side of the ball should be up to discourage a shot, while the other hand should be to the side. When guarding a dribbler, both hands can be to the side.

Figure 2.22
Individual defensive stance.

From the basic stance—body crouched, back straight, knees bent, and weight evenly distributed on both feet, you can best utilize the footwork that will enable you to move quickly to another position that may be required by quick movement of your opponent.

Footwork

Proper defensive footwork centers around the *slide step.* When this step is used, your legs are never crossed and you remain in a position which allows quick changes of direction. Assuming you are sliding right with your opponent, your first movement would be with your right foot, sliding it approximately twelve inches to your right. Your next move would be to slide your left foot into a position very close to your right. Your right foot would then be moved again and so on. The reverse would be true for the slide left (fig. 2.23).

Defensive footwork is similar to that employed by a boxer. To approach an opponent, you simply slide forward, keeping one foot in advance of the other. To defend a drive or cut, use the slide to retreat backwards toward the basket. Remember, to be able to slide properly, your weight must be kept low, balance must be maintained, and your legs should never be crossed.

Position

No matter how correct your stance or how quick your footwork may be, it will be to no avail if you do not maintain proper floor position. Generally, this requires you to remain between your opponent and the defensive basket at all times. If you do this, your opponent can be prevented from cutting or driving in a straight line for the basket and you will be in position to harass any attempted shot.

Your actual defensive floor position will vary depending on whether you are guarding an opponent with or without the ball. If you are guarding an opponent who has the ball, you need to remain on a line between that opponent and the basket (fig. 2.24). If you are guarding an opponent without the ball, it is useful to be aware of the "ballside-helpside" concept as far as floor position is concerned. Figure 2.25 illustrates this concept. Player X1 is guarding O1 who has

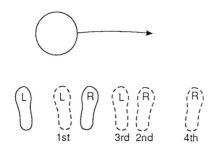

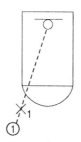

Figure 2.23
The slide step. As the defensive player slides laterally with an opponent, the feet should not cross but slide as shown.

Figure 2.24
Proper defensive position when guarding a player who has the ball. Defensive player X1 should be directly between the offensive player and the basket.

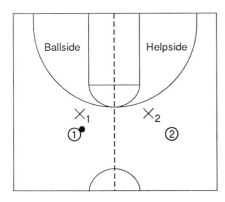

Figure 2.25
The ballside-helpside defensive concept. X1 is guarding O1, who has the ball on the ballside of the court. X2 is guarding O2, who is on the helpside of the court.

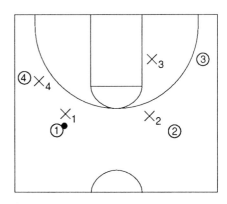

Figure 2.26
X1 and X4 are guarding opponents on the ballside of the court, while X2 and X3 are guarding opponents on the helpside. Notice that X3 is farther away from O3 than X2 is from O2.

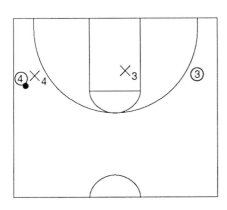

Figure 2.27
O4 has the ball. Notice that X3 has moved even farther away from O3 than in the previous figure.

the ball on the ballside of the court, while X2 is guarding O2 on the helpside of the court. As a general rule, you play close to your opponent on the ballside of the court but considerably off your opponent on the helpside of the court. By playing off your opponent on the helpside, you have more time to react to cuts or screens and are in better position to help your teammate guarding a player on the ballside. When guarding an opponent on the helpside, you play farther away from that opponent the farther the opponent is from the ball. Notice that in figure 2.26 the defender X3 is playing farther off O3 than defender X2 is playing off O2. Player O3 is even farther away from the ball in figure 2.27; therefore X3 sags even farther toward the ballside of the court.

Vision is an important element in individual defense. Where should you focus your eyes while guarding a player with the ball and why? While guarding a player without the ball and why?

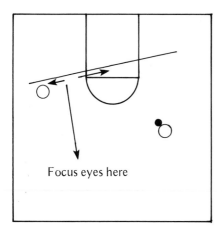

Focus eyes here

Figure 2.28
When guarding an opponent who does not have the ball, the defensive player's eyes should be focused on a point between the ball and the respective opponent. This enables the defensive player to be able to see both the opponent and the ball at the same time and to see other action within an arc of almost 180 degrees.

Vision

Proper vision is as important to defensive play as it is to offensive play. It enables the defensive player to see both the opponent and the ball at the same time. In addition, it enables defensive players to perceive offensive screens and defensive situations that may require their help.

Peripheral vision is important. Players with good eyesight should be able to see action within an arc of almost 180 degrees. By use of peripheral vision, the defensive player should be able to see action both to the left and right.

If the defensive player is guarding an opponent with the ball, the eyes of the defensive player should be focused on the offensive player's belt or midsection. This is very important because the midsection is the only part of the body the offensive player cannot use in faking.

If the defensive player is guarding an opponent who does not have the ball, the eyes should be focused on a spot approximately midway between the opponent and the ball (fig. 2.28). By doing this, peripheral vision will allow the defensive player to see both the opponent and the ball, an important requirement for man-for-man defensive play.

Defensive Talk

Talk on defense is almost as important a fundamental as stance, footwork, and position, yet it often is the most neglected defensive fundamental. Since offensive basketball includes a multitude of screens, cuts, and maneuvers, it is imperative that defensive players communicate with one another to be able to execute proper defensive techniques. Calling out essential terms such as "Ball," "You've got help," "Watch the screen," "Switch," and other defensive terms adds greatly to the effectiveness of team defense.

Figure 2.29
A defensive player attempting to block a jump shot in a game situation.

Figure 2.30
Defensing the jump shooter in a game situation.

Defensive Hints

1. Keep your knees bent, your rear low, and your back almost straight. Your head should remain erect.
2. Stay off your heels.
3. Do not cross your legs when moving across court.
4. Watch the opponent's belt or midsection. It cannot be used to fake.
5. Never leave the floor until after the opponent has gone into the air for the shot.
6. Never turn your head to look for the ball. If you do, your opponent may cut by you to the basket.
7. Prevent your opponent from receiving the ball near the basket.
8. Talk on defense.
9. When your opponents get the ball, *think defense* immediately.
10. Study your opponent. Learn his or her strengths and weaknesses and play accordingly.

Better Players Master These Techniques

3

Mastery of the techniques described in chapter 2 will enable the average individual to enjoy participating in basketball; however, more advanced players master other techniques that enable them to achieve even greater success. Though not absolutely necessary for the average player, a knowledge of and at least minimum skill in these other techniques will increase anyone's enjoyment of the game.

Shooting

The lay-up shot, jump shot, and free throw have become necessary for all players. Another shot used by many advanced players is the *hook* shot.

The Hook Shot

The hook shot is taken from close range and is begun *with the back to the basket.* For a right-hand shot, step onto your left foot and extend your right arm *fully away from your body* with your right hand under the ball in order to achieve control. Keep your left hand on the ball as long as possible (fig. 3.1). As you step

Figure 3.1
The hook shot.

and turn toward the basket, bring your right arm straight upward in a swinging motion toward the basket. Release the ball at the height of the extended arm. Backspin is imparted to the ball as your wrist snaps in a complete follow-through. Most hook shooters shoot the ball against the backboard and let it carom into the goal. The target on the backboard is approximately the same area as for the lay-up shot, some twelve to fifteen inches above the goal.

The hook shot is difficult to master for the average player; however, since the shot is taken with the arm fully extended away from the body, it is so difficult to guard that work on it can pay big dividends in scoring ability, particularly by taller players who play near the basket. The range of the hook shot is limited and it should not be attempted when you are more than ten to twelve feet away from the basket.

Mark a twelve-inch circle on the wall and stand forty feet away. How many times can you hit the target in ten attempts using the baseball pass? Using the hook pass?

Passing

One-Hand Push Pass

Advanced players usually become proficient at passing with one hand. One of the most popular types of one-hand passes is the *one-hand push pass* in which the player—usually a good ball handler—uses one hand simply to push the ball to a teammate. It can be either an air pass or a bounce pass, and it has a definite advantage over the two-hand pass because it can be more easily made from the side of the body. This pass also is very effective off a dribble since it can be passed without the dribbling hand coming in contact with the ball.

Baseball Pass

The baseball pass is used to pass to teammates cutting downcourt and is essential to the repertoire of members of fast-breaking teams. The pass is made with one hand, similar to the regular baseball throw. To begin the pass, bring the ball with the right hand to a position behind your right ear with your weight on your right foot. As you pass downcourt, your weight will shift forward onto your left foot. You should be careful to avoid imparting side spin to the basketball since this makes it curve and decreases accuracy (fig. 3.2).

Hook Pass

The hook pass is sometimes used by advanced players when they are heavily guarded. It is effective when the passer is crowded on one side but there is no pressure on the other side.[1] It is made in the same manner as the hook shot. To hook pass right-handed, step onto your left foot, extend your right arm fully away from your body with your right hand under the ball, and pass the ball in a sweeping motion directly over your head. A wrist snap is important to assure proper follow-through.

Figure 3.2
Starting position for the baseball pass.

The pass is difficult to control; however, it is excellent for passing the ball over an opponent and out to a teammate after a defensive rebound. Like the baseball pass, the hook pass is used quite extensively by fast-breaking teams. The ability to make this pass with either hand adds to your effectiveness.

Dribbling

While all players should learn to dribble with either hand, better players must develop proficiency in three other dribbling techniques:

1. The switch dribble
2. The reverse or spin dribble
3. The change-of-pace dribble

All three techniques are used for changing direction quickly. The switch dribble is faster but does not allow as much protection of the ball as does the reverse dribble.

The Switch Dribble

The switch dribble simply involves changing the hand with which you are dribbling in order to change direction or afford better ball protection. The switch is made in front of your body and must be made as low as possible to prevent the defensive player from deflecting the dribble. As you dribble with your right hand, push the ball sideways in front of your body so that it bounces into position on the left side of your body where it can be taken with your left hand. Your left

Figure 3.3
Beginning the switch dribble.

Figure 3.4
The switch dribble, cont. The ball has been bounced to the floor with the right hand and is about to be received by the left hand.

Figure 3.5
The switch dribble, cont. The ball has been received into the left hand and the dribble is continued.

hand continues the dribble. This skill is essential for a quick change of direction, but since it is done in front of your body, considerable practice is required to be able to protect the ball from the defensive player (figs. 3.3–3.5).

The Reverse Dribble

The reverse or "spin" dribble also makes possible a change of direction; however, throughout the reverse dribble your body is kept between the ball and the defensive player and therefore more protection is given the ball than is possible with

Figure 3.6
Protecting the dribble in a game situation.

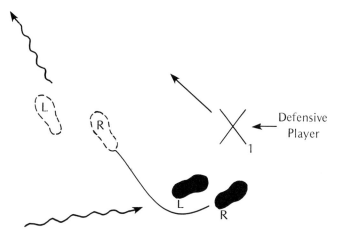

Figure 3.7
Footwork for the reverse or "spin" dribble.

the switch dribble. Since the reverse dribble requires your body to turn 180 degrees in order to execute the change of direction, it is slower than the switch dribble. It usually is used when a defensive player is guarding the dribbler tightly and overplaying in the direction the player is dribbling.

If you are dribbling to your right you must plant your weight on your left foot and swing your right foot in an 180-degree turn while the dribble is being changed to your left hand (fig. 3.7). After the complete turn of the body you will be advancing toward the left and dribbling with your left hand. The accomplished player often can swing his right leg in such a manner as to "trap" the defensive player and thus provide a clear drive to the basket.

The Change-of-Pace Dribble

The change-of-pace dribble technique is simply varying the speed you are moving while dribbling. By varying your speed you keep the defensive player guessing and prevent your opponent from making moves to steal the ball. The change-of-pace is a very good scoring weapon. As you dribble toward the basket at full or near full speed, slow down, coming to almost a complete stop. When the defensive player stops also, you then go at full speed toward the basket. This stop-and-go dribble maneuver often results in letting you drive by your defensive player for an easy lay-up shot.

Dribble Drills

1. *The switch-dribble drill.* Place a chair at the free-throw line. Using your right hand, dribble to the chair. Then switch dribble to your left hand, and drive in for a lay-up shot. Return to the starting position and repeat the drill this time using your left hand first (fig. 3.8).
2. *The reverse-dribble "square" drill.* Start in a corner of the court. Dribble along the sideline to a point even with the free-throw line. Reverse dribble and dribble to the free-throw line. Reverse dribble and dribble along the lane line to the baseline, then reverse dribble and return to the starting point. Repeat this several times using the right hand, then dribble in the opposite direction using the left hand (fig. 3.9).
3. *The "imagination"-dribble drill.* Dribble up and down the court using a variety of dribble moves. Imagine that the defensive player is guarding you. Use the change of pace to get by the defensive player, then use the speed dribble to drive downcourt for a lay-up. On the return trip, use the control dribble to the sideline and, when your imaginary opponent overplays you, reverse dribble and drive downcourt. Use your imagination to enable you to employ all of the dribble moves into a full court game that will not only improve your dribble skills but also will be great for your physical conditioning.

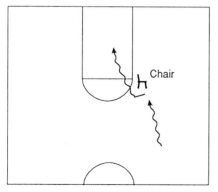

Figure 3.8
A drill to practice the switch dribble.

Chair

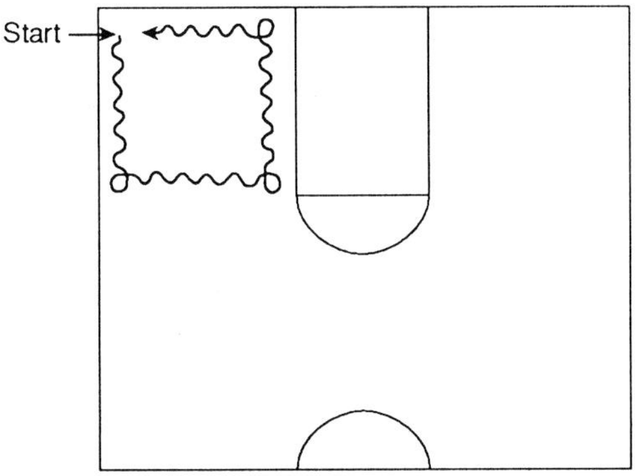

Figure 3.9
The reverse-dribble "square" drill.

The One-on-One Offensive Situation

No matter how well you execute the basic shooting and passing fundamentals, if you do not develop the necessary offensive maneuvers to free yourself from your defensive opponent, you will find it difficult to score. To play "one-on-one," as these maneuvers are commonly called, you need to develop quick starts and stops, fakes and clever changes of direction, and the skill to shoot quickly and from various angles on the court. The ability to play one-on-one does not come easily but requires considerable practice before any degree of success can be achieved against even the average defensive player. Advanced players spend a great deal of time playing one-on-one with each other, and most team offenses provide opportunities for the better players to get their defensive opponents into one-on-one situations.

You should develop the following abilities in order to be a good one-on-one offensive player:

1. *Fake right, shoot.* Fake a drive to your right with a short "jab" step of no more than twelve inches. As the defensive player steps back, go up for the jump shot. It is important that the jab step be short, since a long step will leave you with your feet too wide apart and not in jump-shooting position.
2. *Fake left, shoot.* After a short jab step straight ahead with the right foot, fake your head left as if to drive left. As the defensive player retreats, go up for the jump shot.
3. *Fake right, drive left.* After a short jab step right, immediately drive left without faking the shot.
4. *Fake left, drive right.* Instead of faking right, fake a drive left using your head. As the defensive player moves to your left, drive right.
5. *Fake right, fake left, drive right.* Make a short jab step right, then fake a drive left with your head. As the defensive player moves to your left, drive to the right.
6. *Fake left, fake right, drive left.* Fake a move to the left with your head. Then make a short jab step right. As the defensive player moves to your right, drive to the left using the crossover step illustrated in figure 3.10.

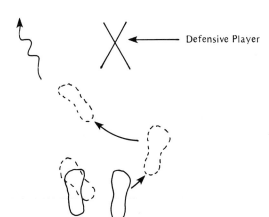

Figure 3.10
The crossover step. With the pivot foot to the left, the offensive player fakes a drive to the right by either stepping to the right or faking the head and shoulders right. Then the offensive player quickly pivots on the left foot an simultaneously crosses the right foot over so the initial step on the drive to the left will be with the right foot.

7. *Fake right, fake shot, drive right.* Make a short jab step right, raise the head and upper body and look at the basket as if you were going to shoot. As the defensive player comes forward, drive to the right.

8. *Fake right, fake shot, drive left.* Make a short jab step right, raise the head and upper body and look at the basket as if you were going to shoot. As the defensive player comes forward, drive to the left using a crossover step.

All of these one-on-one moves are executed before you dribble or at the beginning of your dribble. Therefore, it is important that you not put the ball immediately on the floor after receiving a pass. If you have "used up your dribble" no amount of faking will enable you to drive by your opponent.

The Long First Step

On all of the one-on-one moves described above, an important key to their success is a long first step. After you have made your fake, your first step to the basket must be as long as possible in order to drive you by the defensive player. This is very important, so practice this long step until it becomes automatic.

The Crossover Step

In order to be able to fake one direction and drive another, you must learn the crossover step (fig. 3.10). This step is necessary in order to avoid walking or traveling violations. If the pivot foot is the left foot and you fake right and drive left, your first step left must be made with the right foot; hence the necessity of the crossover step.

Ball Faking

Since the above moves are used at the beginning of a dribble, you must also develop moves to be used at the end of your dribble. Suppose you fake left and drive right toward the basket. Your opponent—diagnosing your moves—moves into proper defensive position. It then will be necessary for you to use additional one-on-one moves to get your shot off. These moves at the end of a dribble center

Figure 3.11
The one-on-one drive in actual play. Player
number 24 has used the crossover step to
drive by the defensive player. Notice that
number 24 is dribbling with the hand away
from the defensive player to better protect
the ball.

around "ball faking." Fake a shot by looking at the basket and faking the ball
at the basket once or twice. The ball fake often will result in the defensive player
leaving the floor too early, and you can jump into the air to shoot after the defender is on the way down. Clever use of ball fakes will enable you to draw fouls,
because the defensive player may fall on you after leaping into the air too early.

*You are closely guarded as you dribble to the left. Which foot must you plant
in order to execute a reverse dribble? Will you turn in a clockwise or
counterclockwise direction?*

Note

1. John R. Wooden, *Practical Modern Basketball,* 3rd ed. (New York: Macmillan Publishing
   Company, 1988), 90.

Progress Can Be Speeded Up

4

In any sport, the mastery of fundamentals is absolutely essential to the development of skill. Basketball is no exception. Fundamentals must be mastered for any degree of playing success. The University of Kentucky's great former coach, Adolph Rupp, said that if there is a secret in successful basketball that secret is drilling on fundamentals.[1] The ability to execute these fundamentals is not learned overnight. Many long hours of work are required; however, progress can be speeded up if a player has a sincere desire to learn basketball skills. Basic is the desire to learn; with that desire, even the less coordinated player can achieve considerable skill—without that desire to learn, even the most athletically inclined will attain little success.

Seek Professional Help and Advice

Players anxious to learn basketball can speed up their progress if they are sure about which skills they should practice, know drills which are recommended for the development of these skills, have a basic understanding of the game, and know when the different skills should be used. These things can best be learned by talking with professional people who are closely associated with the game and by reading the wealth of literature available in books and in athletic coaching journals. Local coaches and physical education instructors will be glad to suggest methods of practicing skills and usually will be able to answer any questions you may have. Accomplished players also can give many helpful hints on how they developed their abilities.

Practice with a Purpose

If progress is to be speeded up, you must practice with a definite purpose in mind. Just going onto a court and shooting a variety of shots for thirty or forty minutes is not enough for quick learning of the basic fundamental skills. Since much of your efforts to develop fundamental skills will be done while practicing alone, you must decide on a definite procedure that will enable you to work diligently on the skills of shooting, passing, dribbling, rebounding, footwork, and individual defense.

A suggested daily practice program follows:

Shooting

1. Warm up by using the alternating-hand lay-up drill. Starting on the right side of the goal, step onto the left foot, and shoot a lay-up shot with the right hand. Take the ball out of the net, step onto the right foot, and shoot a lay-up on the left side of the goal using the left hand. Continue shooting lay-ups on each side of the goal for one minute. How many lay-ups can you make in one minute?
2. Shoot twenty-five driving lay-ups from the right side of the basket and twenty-five driving lay-ups from the left side. Begin at the foul line and, using one dribble with the right hand, drive for a lay-up on the right side of the goal. Retrieve the ball and quickly return to the starting point and repeat. After shooting twenty-five lay-ups with the right hand, shoot twenty-five driving to the left and using the left hand.
3. Shoot a series of jump shots. Start close to the basket shooting ten close jump shots and work out past the foul line. Shoot approximately twenty-five shots from a stationary position without a dribble, then shoot the next seventy-five shots after taking a quick dribble right or left. Count how many shots you make and keep an accurate daily record so that you can check your improvement.
4. Shoot fifty free throws. Count how many you make and record your score. These free throws can be shot as a rest period during some of the other more tiring drills.

Dribbling

1. Using the speed dribble, dribble downcourt and back five times.
2. Using the switch-dribble drill described in the previous chapter, drive for twenty lay-ups with the left hand and twenty lay-ups with the right hand.
3. Place a chair at the free-throw line. Dribble with the right hand to the chair, use the reverse or spin dribble, and drive for a lay-up with the left hand (fig. 4.1). After twenty lay-ups with the left hand, move the chair to the opposite side, make the reverse dribble with the left hand, and drive for right-hand lay-ups.
4. Using the "imagination"-dribble drill, make five trips the full length of the court and back.

Passing

1. Find a smooth wall of the gymnasium. Stand ten or twelve feet from the wall. Using the two-hand chest pass, pass the ball off the wall for three minutes. Change to the bounce pass for another three minutes. This can afford both passing and receiving practice.
2. Make a target on the wall similar to that shown in figure 4.2. The center square counts three points, the next square two points, and the largest square one point. Make ten passes at the target recording the score on each pass. What was your total score? As proficiency is developed, move farther away from the target and use the baseball or hook pass.

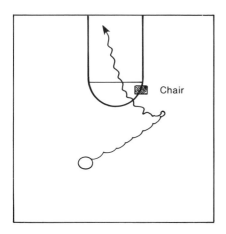

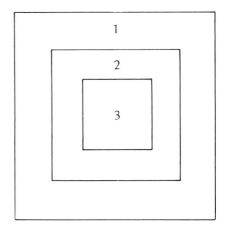

Figure 4.1
The reverse-dribble drill.

Figure 4.2
A passing target. The inside square counts three points, the next square two points, and the largest square one point.

Rebounding

1. Using only one hand, tip the ball against the backboard twenty times with the right hand and twenty times with the left hand.
2. Throw the ball against the backboard, spring into the air as high as possible, and rebound it with two hands. Repeat this twenty-five times.
3. "Superman" rebounding drill. Stand on the lane line on the right side of the basket. Throw the ball high against the backboard so it will rebound on the opposite side of the basket. Move quickly across the lane and jump into the air to rebound the ball. Now, throw the ball on the backboard so it will rebound on the right side. Move quickly across the lane to rebound it. Keep throwing the ball back and forth against the board in this manner for one minute. It will give you a good physical workout and at the same time help develop your lateral jumping ability.

Footwork

1. Beginning at the top of the circle, work on the various one-on-one footwork techniques described in chapter 3. Spend fifteen minutes daily on these maneuvers.

Individual Defense

1. Get into a crouched defensive position. Hold this position for one minute. Increase your time daily until you can stay in defensive position for five minutes.
2. From a crouched defensive position, and using the basic footwork necessary for good defensive play, slide forward, backward, left, and right as quickly as possible without crossing the feet. Start with slides for one minute and increase until you can slide step for five minutes daily.

The big key in developing skills is *diligent practice*. This requires work; there is no substitute for work in any sport, especially if advanced skill is desired. Practice daily! If the gymnasium is not always available, most communities have outdoor hard-surfaced courts that afford adequate practice areas. It would be wise to purchase a rubber basketball for use on these outdoor courts. If no court is available, it is rather economical to purchase a goal and backboard and erect these at your home.

Take Advantage of Every Opportunity to Play

Skills are of no use unless they can be used in actual competitive situations. The ability to pass the ball accurately is no good if you cannot pass it by a defensive player. The ability to shoot accurately is of no use if you do not develop the ability to free yourself from your opposing guard. One other player is all that is necessary for a competitive situation. Play as much one-on-one as possible. The more one-on-one play you can obtain, the quicker you will develop your overall basketball skills.

One-on-one play, however, is not enough. Team play is necessary for success. Three-on-three is excellent for developing both individual and team basketball skills.

Do not neglect five-on-five play. If possible, register for play in intramural leagues or participate on junior varsity teams. If these are not available, investigate the possibility of playing in local city recreation leagues, YMCA or YWCA leagues, and church leagues. Diligent practice is essential, but playing on actual teams is equally important.

Watch Games and Films

An excellent method of learning is to watch games in which accomplished participants are playing. If a college or professional team is nearby, seize every opportunity to see them play. Watch individual players and study their techniques. Study team strategies and patterns in order to achieve a clearer understanding of the game. If no college or professional team is nearby, watch local high-school teams—they too will present good opportunities for learning.

Films provide another excellent avenue for learning the game. All of the college and professional teams and many high-school teams have film available that they are usually willing to lend for the publicity value. Do not hesitate to write to coaches of the various teams for help in securing these game films.

However, the easiest method for obtaining film is to develop your own film library by using a VCR to record college and professional basketball games. Hundreds of college and professional games are shown on television each year. Recording some of these key games and studying them closely on replay can be an invaluable tool in helping you learn the game.

Keep in Good Physical Condition

Since you will run about three miles during an average basketball game, you must have a great deal of strength and endurance, especially in your legs. Following are some recommended exercises that will help you achieve optimum physical condition:

1. *Cross-country running.* Develop the ability to run for several miles up and down hills and over all sorts of terrain. Start out with a short distance and gradually increase the distance until you can run at least three miles without stopping.
2. *Wind sprints.* While cross-country running is great for your endurance, running wind sprints not only aids endurance but helps you increase your speed as well. Run short dashes (fifty-yard) as hard as you can, then walk a similar distance before running another dash at full speed. Continue for several sprints.
3. *Rope jumping.* Rope jumping is very good for endurance and leg strength and also helps develop your coordination and footwork.
4. *Fingertip push-ups.* Do push-ups off the fingertips. This will strengthen your fingers and the muscles used in shooting and passing. In addition, it will reduce finger injuries, a common basketball injury.
5. *Bench jump.* Stand beside a bench approximately sixteen to eighteen inches high. Jump over it and without stopping return to the starting position. Continue jumping over the bench twenty to twenty-five times with stopping. Rest briefly, then repeat. This exercise will add leg strength and increase your jumping ability.
6. *Stops and starts.* Sprint forward, stop, sprint forward. Continue.
7. *Backward running.* Run backward. This not only will help in your conditioning but improve your body balance as well.
8. *Squeeze a ball.* A tennis ball or rubber ball is all you need. Squeeze it for five to ten minutes daily to increase finger and lower-arm strength.
9. *Weight training.* Strength and body bulk is important to basketball players, both male and female, and particularly to those who play near the basket. An organized program of weight training can help your overall physical condition and add strength and necessary weight. Your coach or physical education instructor can recommend certain weight-training exercises for you. Those exercises most often used by basketball players are:
   a. Toe raises
   b. Half squats
   c. Military press
   d. Bench press
   e. Arm curls

Get a Proper Warm-Up Before Practice

Your body can be in peak condition yet be susceptible to injury. To help prevent injuries, make certain to engage in a proper warm-up before every practice period. Jogs around the court and stretching types of exercises prior to any practice that requires quick starts, stops, and jumping are excellent activities. Remember, it is difficult to achieve speedy progress if your body is hampered by a pulled muscle or similar injury.

Take Care of Your Feet

It has often been said that a basketball player is no better than his or her feet. How true! The sudden starts and stops required by the game often result in blisters and foot injuries to those who do not take proper care of their feet. To help prevent these types of injuries, it is very important that you wear shoes and socks that fit properly, and that they be kept as clean as possible. When you feel the beginning of a blister, rub Vaseline on the area to eliminate further friction.

Note

1. Adolph F. Rupp, *Rupp's Championship Basketball* (Englewood Cliffs, N.J.: Prentice Hall, Inc., 1948), 23.

Offensive Patterns of Play

5

Basketball is a team game that requires a great deal of cooperation among players for successful execution of team offensive patterns. In efforts to find offenses difficult to defend against, intelligent coaches have developed a variety of team offenses. The more common are discussed in this chapter.

Major Essentials for a Sound Team Offense

The major essentials necessary for a sound team offense are

1. Movement of the ball
2. Movement of the players
3. Obtaining the good shot
4. Obtaining the second shot
5. Maintaining floor balance
6. The one-on-one situation

Movement of the Ball

All offenses must move the ball if the defense is to be penetrated. This is true whether the defense is man-for-man, zone, or a combination of both. The team that passes the ball slowly from one player to another is simply playing into the hands of the defense, providing an opportunity for the defense to shift, sag, fight through or around screens, or make some other move to counteract an offensive screen or maneuver. On the other hand, the team that keeps the ball moving from player to player will make the defense keep constantly on the move to compensate. It is far easier to attack the defense when it is kept moving than when it is allowed to stand virtually motionless and concentrated around the basket.

Movement of the Players

One of the qualities that often distinguishes great players from good ones is the ability to be dangerous when not in possession of the ball. Most players can make an offensive move if they possess the basketball. Far fewer players remain dangerous after giving up ball possession.

The sound offensive pattern will allow for movement of players in conjunction with movement of the ball. Constant movement, fakes, and cuts are necessary. When players remain in one position and pose no offensive threat, most defenses quickly take advantage and use sinking or double-teaming tactics to congest a more dangerous area. This is far more difficult when all offensive players are kept on the move and each constantly poses a threat to the defense.

Obtaining the Good Shot

The sound offense must work for the good percentage shot. Few teams win consistently if they continually violate this principle. The team that is overly anxious to shoot and has poor play patterns, which result in sub-par team play, will find its members taking the bad shot often—and will find themselves on the short end of the score at game's end.

The sound offensive pattern will be designed so its primary objective is to get the good shot.

Obtaining the Second Shot

Many coaches maintain that this is the chief essential of offensive play. Statistics show that the team that consistently gets the offensive rebound and the resulting second shot attempt usually is successful. Therefore, the offensive pattern must be planned so that at least three players are in position to rebound a shot attempt. Three rebounders in position, provided these players are grounded soundly in offensive rebounding fundamentals, will usually result in an adequate number of second-shot attempts. Obviously, the play patterns should be so designed as to get the better rebounders into the rebounding area.

Maintaining Floor Balance

All good offensive patterns will eliminate congestion insofar as possible. To do this, the floor must be kept balanced. The type of offense being played will determine just where players must be to keep the floor balanced. In general, when two or three players are standing close together (unless part of a play pattern as on a single or double screen), they are easily defensed. One player can defense two standing close together and allow one defensive player to sag and congest the scoring area. Proper floor spacing or balance will help prevent this.

Proper floor balance not only includes offensive balance but defensive balance as well. Provision must be made in every play pattern for players to remain out to prevent fast-break opportunities by the opponents. Of course, the number of players needed for defensive balance responsibilities will depend on the particular opponent. A fast-breaking opponent will require two players back for maintenance of defensive balance, whereas the slow-breaking or ball-control opponent will require only one player back for proper defensive balance.

The One-on-One Situation

The sound offense will include opportunities for the one-on-one situation in order to take advantage of the scoring abilities of the better offensive players and capitalize on weak defensive players. The offensive guard who fakes a drive and shoots the jumper, the forward who drives the baseline for a lay-up, and the center who rolls for a score are all executing one-on-one scoring maneuvers. The stereotyped offense that does not allow such individual scoring moves is greatly reducing its effectiveness and can be scouted and defensed more easily.

Offensive Patterns Against the Man-for-Man Defense

The Single-Post Offense

Figure 5.1 depicts the single-post offense, one of the most common offensive patterns for attacking the man-for-man defense. A and B are the guards, C the center, and D and E the forwards. The guards usually are smaller than the forwards and centers, but generally are better ball handlers and quicker and better outside shooters. The forwards and centers, as a rule, are taller players and do more shooting around the basket and handle a great part of the rebounding responsibilities.

Three simple plays from the single post formation are shown in figures 5.2, 5.3, and 5.4. Of course, they can be run from either side of the court and either guard can initiate the offense. The play shown in figure 5.2 is a simple one involving a center screen for the offside forward. The play diagramed in figure 5.3 is what is commonly called a split-the-post play, while the play shown in figure 5.4 is the second-guard play that was popularized by famed coach Adolph Rupp while at the University of Kentucky.

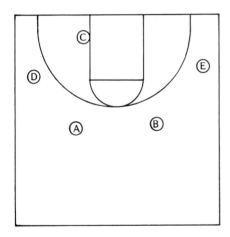

Figure 5.1
Basic single-post offensive formation.

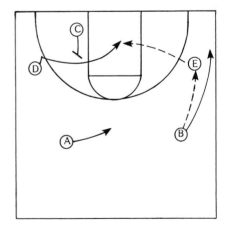

Figure 5.2
Single-post play. Player B passes to E, who passes to D, cutting off screen set by C.

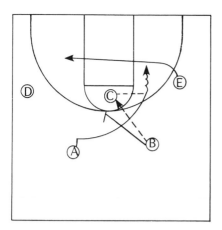

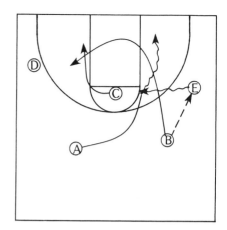

Figure 5.3

A single-post play using the high post. E clears to the left side as B passes to C. Then B cuts off C, and A cuts around using B as a screen. A receives pass from C and drives for a lay-up or jump shot. This is referred to as a split-the-post play.

Figure 5.4

The "Kentucky second-guard" play from the single post. B passes to E and clears through.

E drives to the free-throw line and gives a flip pass to A, who drives for a lay-up or jump shot.

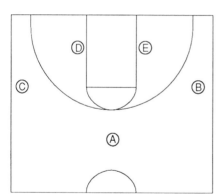

Figure 5.5

Basic double-post offensive formation.

The Double-Post Offense

The double-post offense is shown in figure 5.5. This offense is used when a team has two tall players they would like to keep close to the basket, and three smaller players who can handle the ball well and shoot from the outside. A is the point guard, B and C are the wing players, and D and E are the post players.

Figures 5.6, 5.7, and 5.8 show three simple plays from the double-post formation. Figure 5.6 is a split-the-post play, while figure 5.7 is a double screen for a wing player.

Figure 5.8 shows a play involving a cross screen for one of the post players.

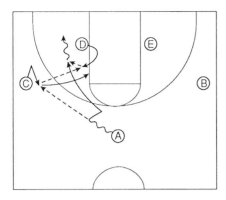

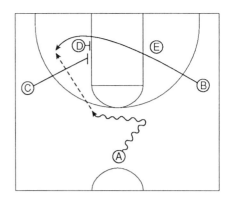

Figure 5.6

A split-the-post play from a double-post formation. A passes to C who passes to D. C cuts toward the basket while A cuts outside for a pass from D. The cuts by C and A should be timed so the cut by C sets a natural screen for A.

Figure 5.7

C and D set a double screen for B. A dribbles right to set up the defense, then reverse into position for a pass to B.

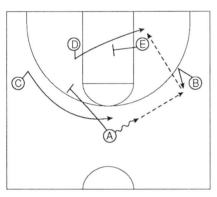

Figure 5.8

A cross screen for a post player. A passes to B and screens C as E sets the screen for D. B can pass to D under the basket or to C, who will reverse the ball to the other side of the court.

The High-Low Post or 1–3–1 Offense

A third type of offensive pattern is illustrated in figure 5.9 and is referred to as the "high-low post" or 1–3–1 offense. A is the point guard, B and C are the wing players, D is the high-post player, and E is the low-post player.

Figures 5.10, 5.11, and 5.12 show simple plays from this formation. Figure 5.10 illustrates a simple screen on the ball with a double-screen option, while figure 5.11 shows a double screen for the low-post player. A double-screen play for a wing player is shown in figure 5.12.

Can you list the three main requirements for a "good" shot?

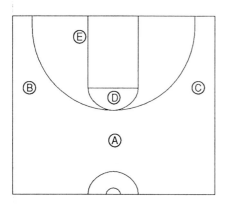

Figure 5.9
Basic high-low post or 1-3-1 offense.

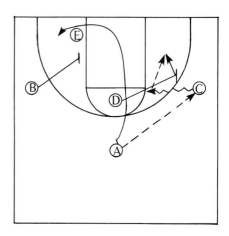

Figure 5.10
A passes to C and cuts off D, who is looking for a possible pass from C. After A cuts by, D moves out to set a screen for C. As C dribbles off the screen, B and E are setting a double screen for A. C may shoot or drive to the basket, pass to D on a roll play, or pass to A behind the double screen.

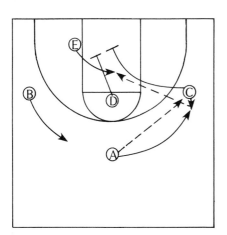

Figure 5.11
A passes to C and cuts outside to take a return pass. C and D move across the lane to set a double screen for E.

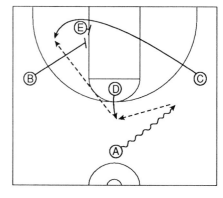

Figure 5.12
A dribbles toward C as B and E form a double screen for C. A passes to D popping out to the top of the circle. D passes to C behind the double screen.

The Shuffle Offense

A pattern-type offense simply called the "shuffle" was developed by Bruce Drake while he was head coach at the University of Oklahoma. It is a unique offense since players must learn to play all five positions. Because of this fact, the shuffle is a particularly strong offense for a team not possessing the good tall player but which has balanced height.

If all team members are similar in height, which type of offense might be particularly good to try? Does this offense require more or less player versatility than the single-post offensive formation?

Figure 5.13 shows the initial formation of the shuffle attack. Note that the player in each position has a specific number. Number 3 passes to 2 who passes to 1. Number 3 cuts off the screen set by the post player 5. This is referred to as the first option. As 3 cuts into the pivot area, 4 makes a V cut on the baseline and cuts high toward the ball into a more or less second option position. After passing to 1, 2 sets a screen for 5, who cuts to the top of the circle for a possible pass from 1. This is the third option. If no shot is obtained as a result of this play, the players are now in the position shown in figure 5.14, and are ready to run the offense from the right side of the floor. The reader can quickly see that one of the distinct advantages of this pattern is the fact that the players do not have to return to their original starting positions to continue the offense.

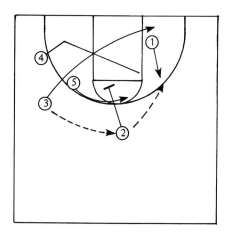

Figure 5.13
Basic shuffle offense. Pattern begins with overload to one side, in this case left. Number 3 passes to 2 who passes to 1. Number 3 cuts off 5's screen. Number 4 then cuts as shown toward the ball. Number 5 moves to top of circle off 2's screen.

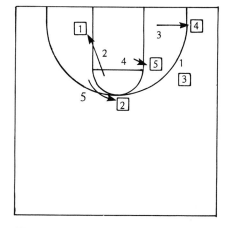

Figure 5.14
Shuffle continuity. After the cuts diagrammed in figure 5.13 have been made, players will be overload to the right side of the court and ready to continue the pattern. Here, 3 has the ball and will pass to 2 who will relay to 1.

The Flex Offense

An offense that has become very popular in recent years is the "flex" offense. It is an offense similar to the shuffle in that players must learn to play all five positions. Figure 5.15 shows the initial set-up of the offense, with point guard A dribbling the ball into position as B, C, D, and E set up along the baseline. Though the offense can be run both to the left and right, figure 5.16 shows the basic offense initiated by a dribble right and a pass to the left post player D breaking to the side of the free-throw line. On the pass, B cuts off the screen set by E and looks for the lay-up. Player A then sets a screen for E coming to the free-throw line for a possible jump shot. If neither is open, the offense continues as shown in figure 5.17. Player C cuts off the screen set by the initial cutter B. Player D then sets a screen for B cutting to the free-throw line. A patient, well-coached team can continue this pattern until an open shot is obtained.

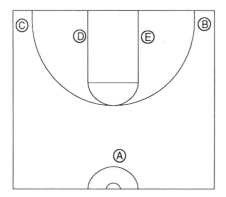

Figure 5.15
Initial formation for the flex offense.

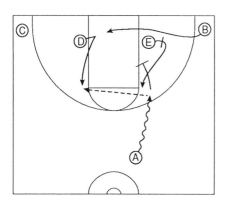

Figure 5.16
Initial cuts of the flex offense. A passes to D as B cuts off the screen sets by E. A then sets a screen for E, who cuts to the free-throw line. This action is referred to as "screening the screener."

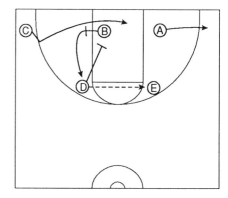

Figure 5.17
Continuation of the flex offense. D passes to E as C cuts off the screen set by the initial cutter B. D then sets a screen for B cutting to the free-throw line.

The Passing Game

The passing game, often referred to as motion offense, has become one of the most predominant offenses in basketball. Henry Iba of Oklahoma State was among the first coaches to use the offense successfully, and Dean Smith has done an excellent job using it with his teams at North Carolina. However, the coach who has done more than any other for the popularity of this offense is Bobby Knight of Indiana University. He has used it to win three NCAA national titles, a Pan-American Games championship, and the 1984 Olympic gold medal.

The passing game is a free-lance type of offense. Players have freedom to move about the court and are not required to cut to certain areas as required by set-play offenses. The offense emphasizes movement of the ball, movement of players, shot selection, and team play. At the same time, it minimizes dribbling and one-on-one individual play. It can be run from any formation.

Though players are given a certain amount of freedom, all passing-game offenses operate within a strict set of rules. It is very important that players know these rules and abide by them, for if players violate them, the offense will turn into a helter-skelter, undisciplined free-lance attack. Some of the rules common to most passing game offenses are:

1. *You must move every time a pass is made.* This may sound simple but it is a rule that is violated often. Players have a tendency to stand still after passing.
2. *Move with a purpose.* When players move, they must move with a purpose, not aimlessly. They move to screen, to cut to the basket looking to get open, or to fake a screen and then cut to the basket, always with a purpose.
3. *Take no more than two dribbles after the offense is initiated.* This helps build up team play and eliminates excessive dribbling and the resulting individual play.
4. *At least four passes must be made before a shot is taken unless the ball goes to the low post area.* Four passes help instill team play and the feeling that if players give up the ball they will get it back.
5. *Anytime players are overplayed by the defense, they must cut to the goal or screen for a teammate.* This rule is important to keep players from "fighting pressure."
6. *Always make the easy pass.* This may sound simple, but it may be the most important rule. What is an easy pass for one player may be a hard pass for another. As players learn to make the easy pass, their turnover rate decreases greatly.
7. *When you pass the ball, either cut for the basket or screen for a teammate.*
8. *After receiving a pass, the player must face the goal and hold the ball at least two seconds before passing.* Players have a tendency to receive the ball and pass too quickly. The two-second pause gives things a chance to develop inside and allows the passer time to see them.
9. *After cutting into the post area, players must move out if they do not receive the ball within two seconds.*

There are several keys to the success of the passing-game offense. They are the following:

1. *Movement of the ball.* It is very important that the ball be kept moving. Each player should hold the ball for two seconds to give things a chance to develop, then the ball should be passed. The more the ball is moved, the more difficult it is for the defense.
2. *Player movement.* We are referring to moving without the ball. It is a basic fundamental skill that players need to learn. Without proper player movement the defense can prevent good ball movement. Both ball movement and player movement are dependent on one another.
3. *Shot selection.* It is absolutely necessary that players take good shots. Excellent ball and player movement will make no difference if a team's shot selection is poor.
4. *Team play.* Since movement of the ball and the players is so important to the passing game's success, team play becomes even more important. Bad shots and individual play will result in poor ball and player movement.

Zone Offense

The offensive patterns shown in figures 5.1 through 5.17 are designed for attacking man-for-man defenses. All teams also must have offensive patterns for attacking the various zone defenses that may be faced.

Generally a team needs two zone-offense attacks, one for an even-front zone defense (2–3, 2–1–2) and one for an odd-front zone defense (1–3–1, 1–2–2).

The 1–3–1 Zone Attack

The most popular attack for the 2–1–2 and 2–3 zone defenses is the 1–3–1 zone offense. Figure 5.18 shows the basic formation for this attack. Player A is the key ball handler and must assume responsibility for directing the attack. B and C should be the team's best shooters, while D should be a good shooter and passer from the high post area. E is the baseline player and should have the ability to score in the low post area.

A variety of plays and scoring options can be used with the 1–3–1 zone offense. Several are suggested in figures 5.19 through 5.25.

The 2–1–2 Zone Attack

The 2–1–2 offensive attack is commonly used against 1–3–1 and 1–2–2 zones. The attack formation is shown in figure 5.26. A and B are the guards and should possess shooting ability from these positions. C and D are the forwards and should be able to shoot from the corner areas. E is the center or best post player.

The basic 2–1–2 attack depends on the zone-attack principles of the 1–3–1 attack—movement of the ball, penetration, skip passing, and good shot selection. Movement of players can occur either in a free-lance manner or with a set pattern as shown by figure 5.27.

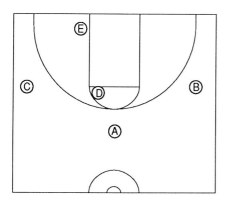

Figure 5.18

The basic formation for the 1-3-1 zone offense. A is the key ball handler and "quarterback."
B and C should be the better shooters, while D and E are the best post players.

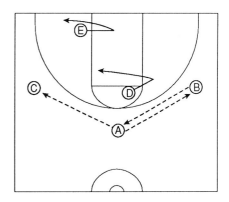

Figure 5.19

Rapid movement of the ball is an important principle in attacking any zone defense. Quick passing from A to B, back to A, then on to C may result in an open shot for C.

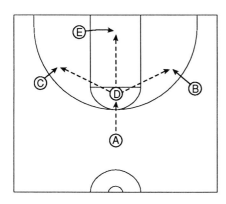

Figure 5.20

The high-post player should be a good passer who can pass the ball to teammates cutting into open areas of the zone.

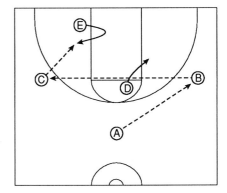

Figure 5.21

The use of the skip pass against a zone defense. A passes to B who passes cross-court to C.
C may have an open shot or be able to pass to E in the low post.

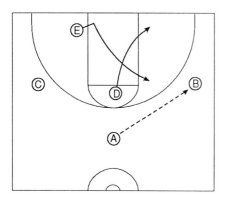

Figure 5.22

Post players D and E may use an X move in an effort to get open inside. As A passes to B, D cuts to the low post as E fills the vacated high-post area.

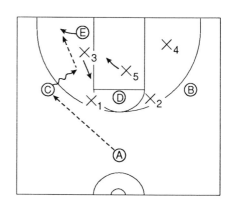

Figure 5.23

The use of penetration to get an open shot. C drives into the area between X1 and X3, forcing both of the defenders to cover. C quickly passes to E on the baseline. This type of penetration can occur between two defenders at any part of the zone and is referred to as "dribbling the gaps" of the zone.

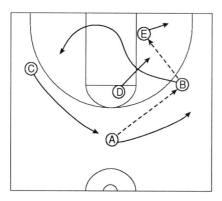

Figure 5.24

Movement of players in the 1-3-1 zone defense. A passes to B who passes to E on the baseline. B cuts through the zone looking for a possible pass back from E. A fills the spot vacated by B, and C fills the spot vacated by A. B will cut to the wing position vacated by C.

Figure 5.25

The use of screens against a zone defense. A dribbles toward B who clears to the opposite side. A passes to high-post D at the top of the circle. D passes to B for a shot behind the double screen set by C and E.

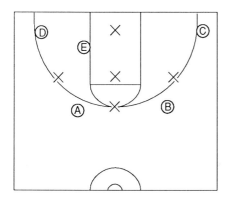

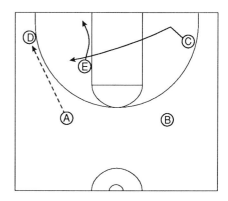

Figure 5.26
The basic 2-1-2 zone attack formation. This example shows the offense against a 1-3-1 zone defense.

Figure 5.27
A player-movement pattern from the 2-1-2 zone offense. As A passes to D, E cuts to the low-post area, and C cuts into the position vacated by E.

The Fast Break

A very popular pattern of play throughout the country is the fast break offense. It is a planned attempt by the offense to get the ball into its scoring area so quickly that its members will outnumber the opposition. Fast break teams hope to rebound a missed shot by the opponent and pass it quickly downcourt as players break at full speed into the scoring area.

The most common fast break situations are the three-on-two and the two-on-one. Occasionally the defense will get caught without anyone back and the offense will get a one-on-none situation. Other outnumbering situations are four-on-three and five-on-four.

Figure 5.28 shows a typical three-on-two fast break pattern. Player A rebounds the ball and tosses it out to player B. Player B passes to the middle to player C and cuts down the right sideline. While this has been taking place, player D has cut hard down the left sideline to fill a lane and the players outnumber the opponents three to two.

The two-on-one situation is illustrated in figure 5.29. Player A rebounds the ball and tosses it out to player B. B advances the ball downcourt and sees that the defense has only one player back. B can either advance the ball downcourt on the dribble or pass it to player C, who advances it downcourt as indicated. As C reaches an area approximately even with the free throw line, C passes the ball to B for the lay-up. Of course, what C does with the ball will be determined by how the lone defender plays. If the defender plays toward B, C may fake the pass and drive for the lay-up. Considerable drill practice in both the three-on-two and two-on-one is necessary for players to be able to react properly.

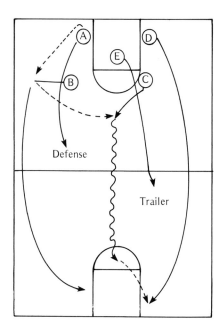

Figure 5.28
Typical three-on-two fast-break pattern.

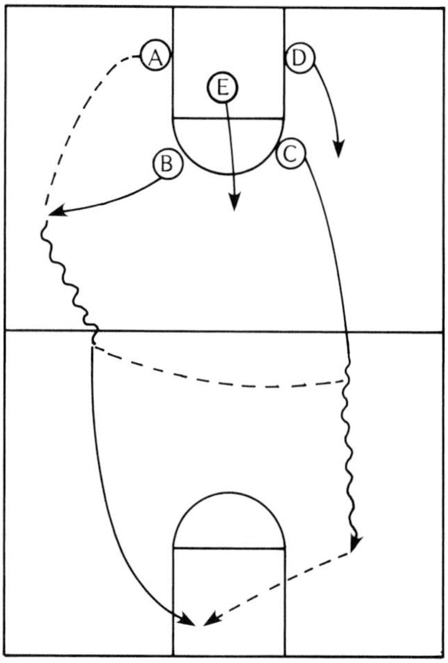

Figure 5.29
A two-on-one fast-break pattern.

The key to the successful fast break is the speed with which the outlet pass is made after a rebound. If the rebounder holds the ball for a few seconds, the defensive team has time to fall back into proper position. On the other hand, if the rebounder quickly passes the ball out to a teammate, good opportunities are presented for them to get the ball down the floor before the opponents have gained defensive position.

The fast break is colorful to watch and enjoyed greatly by the spectators. It is largely responsible for the popularity that professional basketball enjoys today. It is true that moving the basketball at full speed does lead to ball-handling errors. Many coaches, particularly those in junior and senior high schools, feel that the advantages gained by the fast break do not offset the errors made in attempting it; therefore, these coaches do not allow their players to use the fast break as an offensive weapon. However, players love the fast-breaking game and, as they become more and more skilled, it is being used more and more.

When to Fast-Break

Opportunities for the fast break may be found after the following situations:

1. A missed field goal or free throw by the opponents.
2. A successful field goal or free throw by the opponents.
3. A bad pass, double dribble, or other loss of ball possession by the opponents.
4. A jump-ball situation.

The fast break defense is popular with players and spectators but it entails certain risks. Can you name three reasons why this type of defense might fail?

Out-of-Bounds Situations

A team must have special plays to inbound the ball when they have it out-of-bounds either under their basket or along the sideline. The first purpose of the special play is simply to get the ball inbounds; however, as the ball is taken out-of-bounds there is a lapse in the action that affords a good opportunity to call a special play that may result in a score.

Figures 5.30 and 5.31 show two commonly used plays from under the basket, while figures 5.32 and 5.33 show plays used along the sideline.

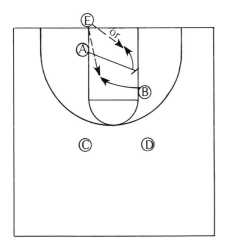

Figure 5.30
A sets a screen for B who cuts toward the ball. If the defense does not switch, the pass is made to B. If the defense switches, the pass is made to A rolling back toward the ball.

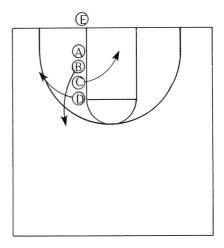

Figure 5.31
Vertical formation. D cuts toward corner. After D cuts, C cuts into the lane. B then moves out to receive pass if D and C are not open.

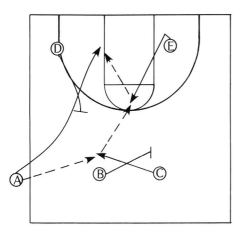

Figure 5.32
B screens for C who receives inbounds pass. C passes to E, who passes to A cutting off the rear screen set by D.

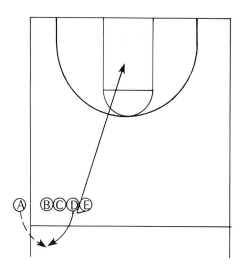

Figure 5.33
Four-in-a-line horizontal formation. Excellent for late in the game when you are leading and the opponent has to have the ball. If closely guarded, E cuts to the basket for possible pass and lay-up. If not closely guarded, E simply breaks into the backcourt to receive inbounds pass.

The Three-Point Shot

In the spring of 1986, the college rules committee added the three-point field goal to college basketball. The following year, the National Federation of High School Athletic Associations followed suit.

The three-point play has become one of the most exciting developments in the game of basketball in many years. Prior to its addition, basketball had become geared to the inside shot, with fewer and fewer outside shots taken each year. Coaches constantly stressed building an offense from the inside-out as opposed to outside-in, and such emphasis had reduced drastically the number of outside shots in each game. There is little question that the high, arching outside shot is the most enjoyable shot in the game for fans and players alike. The three-point shot puts this type of shot back into the game.

The Argument Over Distance

The college rules committee, after considerable experimentation, determined that the distance for the three-point shot would begin at 19' 9", and the high-school committee decided to use that distance also.

Considerable argument ensued after the college committee passed the 19' 9" distance. Many coaches as well as fans felt the distance was too short and expected it to be moved back for the 1987–88 season; however, this did not occur and it is doubtful that the distance will be changed in the near future.

Advantages of the Three-Point Shot

1. The shot counts *three* points instead of two. (This is the most obvious advantage.)
2. It enables a team to catch up more quickly.
3. It tends to open the post area for better post play.

4. It puts outside shooting back into the game.
5. It gives an opportunity for players who may not be as physically skilled as others to make positive contributions to a team.
6. It increases offensive rebounding opportunities.
7. It increases fan interest.
8. Players like the three-point shot.
9. It decreases the advantage of a zone defense.

Disadvantages of the Three-Point Shot

1. A team's shooting percentage will vary more than with the two-point shot.
2. Players who are not good three-point shooters may waste time practicing the three-point shot.
3. Teams may exhibit a lack of offensive patience.
4. Quick three-point shots may tend to make a team look like a "playground" team.
5. Teams may neglect the inside game.

Techniques for Getting the Three-Point Shot

There are a number of techniques that can be included in offensive play patterns to obtain a good three-point shot:

1. Penetration and pitch (fig. 5.34).
2. Rear screen and step out (fig. 5.35).
3. Single and double screens.
4. Ball movement inside-out. When the ball is passed to a post player inside and the defense drops to double-team, the post player can pass to an open three-point shooter.

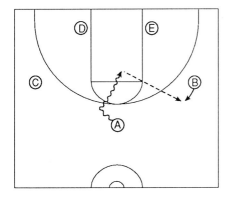

Figure 5.34
Penetration by A toward the basket forces the defense to collapse and enables a pass to B for a three-point-shot attempt.

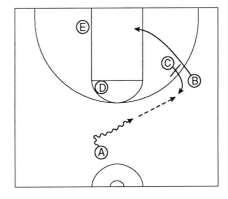

Figure 5.35
Rear screen and step out for a three-point-shot opportunity. C sets rear screen for B. As the defender guarding C steps back to help on the cut by B, C can step out for the shot.

5. The skip pass. The skip pass from one side of the court to the other has always bothered zone defenses and becomes even more effective for the three-point shot.

6. Fast break. Some of the better three-point opportunities will come off a fast-break type of situation.

Special Three-Point Plays

Figures 5.36 and 5.37 show two special plays that can be used to obtain a three-point shot. Both plays involve a double screen for the shooter. One play is from the single-post offense and the other from the 1–3–1 offense.

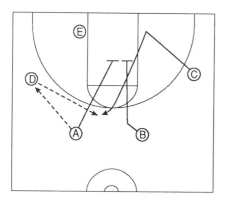

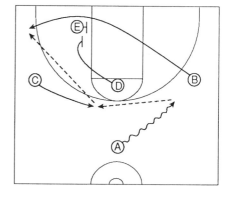

Figure 5.36
A passes to D and joins B in setting up a double screen for C cutting to the top of the circle for a three-point shot.

Figure 5.37
A dribbles toward the sideline and reverse passes to C, who passes to B cutting off a double screen set by D and E.

Defensive Patterns of Play

6

The importance of sound team defensive play in championship basketball cannot be overemphasized. The major difference between the average basketball team and those who ride the crest of the tournament trail at the end of the season lies in the ability to play defense!

There are basically two different types of defenses: the man-for-man defense, and the zone defense. The man-for-man defense assigns a player a specific opponent to guard and this opponent must be guarded wherever the opponent may go in the opponent's offensive pattern. In the zone defense, the defensive player is assigned an area or zone on the court to guard rather than a particular opponent. The defensive player then guards any opposing player who comes into this zone or area.

Though the man-for-man and zone are basically the two defenses in basketball, they have been combined; different shifts and maneuvers have been employed with each. The result is quite a number of different defenses used in the game.

Team Defensive Essentials

Regardless of the type of defense a team may use, certain essentials must be adhered to for the defense to be successful:

1. *Team members must have a desire to play defense.* Because of the nature of the game and the tremendous amount of publicity and public favor given to the high scorers, most players prefer to play offense. However, defense can be the great equalizer. When the offense is having a bad night—and this will invariably happen—good sound defense can produce victory. But good sound defense cannot be played unless team members want to play defense.

2. *Correct defensive stance and footwork must be used by all team members.* No player can play good defense in an incorrect stance or with faulty footwork. Since a good team defense is dependent on not one or two players but on five working as a coordinated unit, improper stance or footwork by any one of the five can reduce greatly the effectiveness of the team defense.

In making specific player assignments for man-for-man defense, what are the factors that should be considered?

3. *Correct positioning must be maintained by all team members.* A player cannot expect to defense an opponent unless proper floor position is maintained. In man-for-man defenses, this will mean that the defensive player

usually will be between the respective opponent and the basket. If the opponent breaks into the dangerous area near the basket, it will be necessary for the defender to play between this opponent and the ball to prevent the opponent from receiving the ball in such a dangerous scoring position. If the team defense is a zone, each defender must be in the proper floor position in the assigned zone and must make the proper shifts with the movement of the ball. An incorrect shift will result in improper floor position and a weakness in the team defense. One player out of position can nullify the work of four other players and weaken an otherwise sound defensive unit.

4. *Team members must talk to one another to be able to combat the variety of situations that may occur.* Talk is a valuable asset to a good team defense. The player who will not yell out to teammates to warn them of special situations will impair the effectiveness of the team defense, despite being a good individual defensive player. Calls, such as "watch the screen," "screen left," "switch," "stay," "rebound," and "slide through" are a few of the many needed to insure correct defensive action for the variety of offensive screens and maneuvers that may be faced.

5. *Definite responsibilities and techniques must be established for meeting the various types of offensive maneuvers that may be encountered.* A good team defense will be prepared to meet all types of offensive formations whether it be a single-post, double-post, or other offensive formation. Definite techniques and responsibilities must be established for meeting the various play patterns that go toward making up these team offenses. Definite methods are necessary for handling the various types of screens, the split-the-post situation, the give-and-go, the screen-and-roll, the double screen, and other offensive plays. These methods must be developed on the practice floor and cannot be left to chance during the game.

6. *Definite rebounding assignments must be made.* Rebounding assignments begin with a shot by the opponent. If the defense is a man-for-man, all defensive players must screen (box out) their opponents so that they will be between their respective opponent and the basket. Failure to do this by any one member of the defense can result in an easy basket for the opponent. If the defense is a zone, players must be certain of rebounding areas and must attempt block-outs of opponents in their respective areas.

B has the ball. The defense is sagging to prevent a pass to E. What should B do with the ball? What is a good way to get the ball to E?

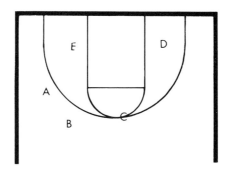

Man-for-Man Defense

Use of the man-for-man defense permits defensive assignments to be made on the basis of height, position, speed, and offensive ability. The team's best defensive guard may be assigned to the opponent's best-scoring guard. The poorest defender may be assigned the opponent's weakest scorer. A slow defensive player may be assigned a slow opponent. Thus match-ups are facilitated and definite responsibility can be charged for scoring by opponents. Individual pride in defensive ability is thereby more easily fostered since each player has a particular opponent to guard and can be judged by how many points that opponent scores.

General Principles for Man-for-Man Team Defense

Most teams that use the man-for-man defense will use general team defensive principles similar to the following:

1. *Maintain a position between your opponent and the basket unless the opponent is in the pivot area close to the basket.*
2. *Always "pressure" the ball.* One defensive player must be closely guarding the player with the ball at any time that player is within shooting distance.
3. *Protect the baseline.* Most man-for-man defenses concentrate on preventing opponents from driving along the baseline to the basket. For a number of years this was a cardinal rule of *all* man-for-man defenses. However, in recent years there have been a number of teams, including Indiana University and North Carolina, which have built their defenses by actually forcing the offensive player to drive the baseline. For the average team it is, nevertheless, better to protect the baseline from the driver.
4. *Prevent the close shot.* Good man-for-man defensive clubs seldom give up the open lay-up shot. When a driver gets by an opponent and moves for the basket, the driver is no longer the responsibility of one player but becomes the responsibility of *all* defensive players. Defensive players must then converge on the basket in efforts to prevent the close shot.
5. *Prevent the second shot.* The game can be won or lost on the backboards. It is mandatory for all defensive players to screen their respective opponents off the board in order to minimize the number of rebounds and resulting second shots the offense may obtain.
6. *Screens must be handled with consistency.* This means that a team must practice prior to game play the method it will use in combating screens. If switching is to be used against screens, then switching techniques must be practiced. Figure 6.1 illustrates a common switching maneuver. If players are not to switch, then they must practice fighting through screens and receiving help from their teammates as shown in figure 6.2.
7. *Keep the ball out of the pivot area.* Once a player receives a pass in the pivot area close to the basket, it is virtually impossible to defense that player. Therefore, it is imperative that such passes be prevented.

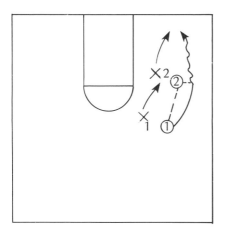 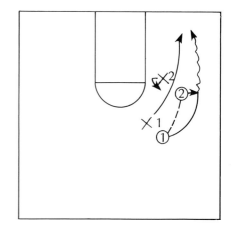

Figure 6.1
A common switching maneuver by a man-to-man defense. O1 passes the ball to O2, receives a return pass, and drives to the baseline. X2 simply yells "switch" and picks up O1 driving to the baseline. X1 guards O2.

Figure 6.2
The same offensive maneuver with the defense not switching. As O1 cuts outside, X2 simply takes a step back and lets X1 slide through and keep O1.

Defensive Positioning

In order to maintain correct defensive position, players should be constantly aware of the ballside-helpside concept as presented in chapter 2 (fig. 2.25). Normal man-for-man defensive positions with the ball at the guard position are illustrated in figure 6.3. Players X2 and X4 are guarding ballside players and thus are close to their respective opponents, with X2 pressuring the ball. Defenders X1, X3, and X5 are guarding opponents on the helpside of the court and therefore are playing off and toward the ball in a "helping" position.

The ball is shown at the forward position in figure 6.4. Player X4 is pressuring the ball while X1, X3, and X5 have moved farther toward the ballside of the court. X2 has jumped toward the ball and is discouraging a pass to 02.

The position on the court in which defensive players pick up their opponents can vary. Figures 6.3 and 6.4 show the normal man-for-man defense. However, the pickup position can be moved out to the midcourt line, in which case the defense is referred to as the *half-court man-for-man press* (fig. 6.5). Going farther, the position of pickup can be made at three-quarter or at full court and the defense referred to as the *three-quarter-court man-for-man press,* or the *full court man-for-man press* (figs. 6.6, 6.7).

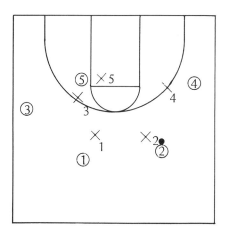

Figure 6.3
Normal man-for-man defensive positioning with the ball at the guard position.

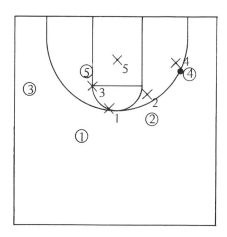

Figure 6.4
Normal man-for-man defensive positioning with the ball at the forward position.

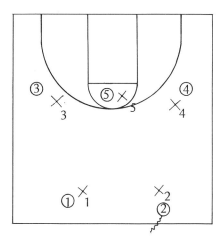

Figure 6.5
The half-court man-for-man press. Defensive players stay very close to their assigned opponents and, when the dribbler picks up the ball, all defensive players try to prevent passes to the players they are guarding.

Pressing defenses are used in an effort to force the opponent to make mistakes. Such defenses are particularly useful against a weak-ball-handling team, an inexperienced team, a poorly conditioned team, and especially against a methodical-pattern-type team. It is an absolute must when the defensive team is trailing late in the game.

Rather than pressing, the man-for-man defense might sag and jam the defensive basket area. This is referred to as a sagging man-for-man defense or collapsing man-for-man defense. This type of man-for-man defense is used quite often when an opposing team is weak in outside shooting or has a high-scoring center.

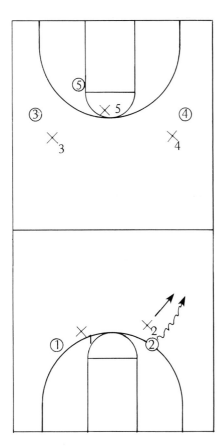

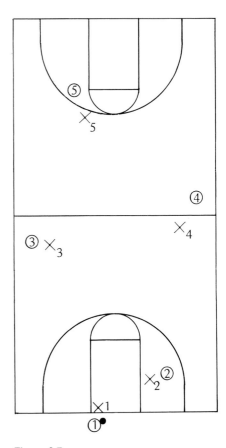

Figure 6.6
The three-quarter-court man-for-man press. Defensive players attempt to prevent passes to the player they are guarding.

Figure 6.7
The full-court man-for-man press. Defensive players pick up their opponents while the ball is still out-of-bounds.

Zone Defense

Zone defenses differ from man-for-man defenses in that players are assigned a particular area of the court to defend rather than having to defense a specific opponent. Foremost attention is focused on the ball and the area of the court to be defended. All defensive players mass in assigned areas in and around the free throw lane and shift as a coordinated unit with each movement of the ball by the offense. This team massing and shifting protects the area close to the basket and makes short shots difficult to obtain.

In what court area is the opponent normally picked up in zone defense? How may the position of pick-up vary? Is the possible area of pick-up different for man-for-man defense?

Advantages of Zone Defense

1. It effectively counters the set-pattern offense involving screening and cutting.
2. It affords maximum protection in the area close to the basket, making short shots difficult to obtain.
3. Fouls are committed less frequently. A switch to a zone defense is often wise when a key player has accumulated several fouls.
4. It conserves energy.
5. Fast breaks are more easily obtained from zone formations.
6. Most zone defenses strengthen rebounding.
7. It is very effective on small courts so often used by high-school, YMCA, and recreation-league teams.
8. It minimizes fundamental mistakes by a poor defensive player.
9. It increases chances for pass interceptions and encourages "ball-hawking."
10. It is relatively easy to learn.

Disadvantages of Zone Defense

1. It is weak against good outside-shooting teams. The advent of the three-point shot makes this an even bigger disadvantage.
2. It is susceptible to fast-breaking teams.
3. It allows opponents to overload an area by placing two players in the area guarded by one defensive player.
4. Individual defensive fundamentals tend to be weakened.
5. It is often ineffective against the deliberate game or stall. When a team is behind in the score late in the game, the standard zone defense must be abandoned.

General Principles for Zone Defense

1. *Players must get into position quickly.* Most offensive plans for defeating the zone include the fast break. Therefore, zone defensive players must hustle downcourt and into proper defensive position immediately upon giving up the ball.
2. *Players must maintain good individual defensive stance.* The rapid shifts necessary with offensive ball movement can be executed more quickly when proper defensive stance is maintained. In addition, correct stance is necessary to prevent offensive dribble penetration.
3. *Players should keep hands up in position to deflect passes.*
4. *Talk is of utmost importance to be able to handle offensive movement.*
5. *Players must focus their attention on the ball and shift rapidly with each movement of the ball.* Zone defensive players should never turn their backs to the ball.
6. *Prevent the second shot.* This principle is of no less importance in the zone defense than in the man-for-man defense. Zone players must know their rebounding responsibilities regardless of where a shot may be taken.

Types of Zone Defenses

Four major zone defenses are used by modern basketball teams:

1. 2–1–2 zone
2. 2–3 zone
3. 1–3–1 zone
4. 1–2–2 zone

These zone defenses are pictured in figures 6.8 through 6.13. Zone defenses require that the players move in their area according to the position of the ball. This movement is referred to as *shifting*. Note in figures 6.9 and 6.10 how the 2–1–2 zone has shifted as the ball is passed around the perimeter of the defense. This shifting is necessary in all types of zone defenses.

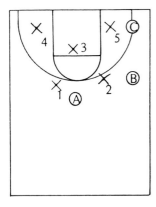

Figure 6.8
The 2-1-2 zone defense.

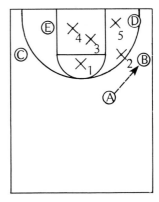

Figure 6.9
The shift of the 2-1-2 zone with the ball at the forward position.

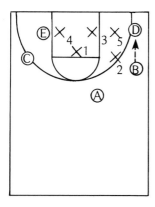

Figure 6.10
The shift of the 2-1-2 zone with the ball in the corner.

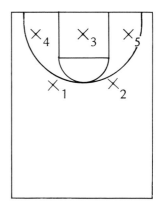

Figure 6.11
The 2-3 zone defense.

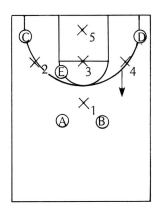

Figure 6.12
The 1-3-1 zone defense.

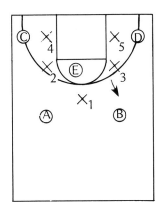

Figure 6.13
The 1-2-2 zone defense.

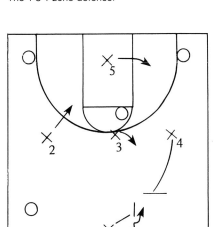

Figure 6.14
The 1-3-1 half-court zone press. As the dribbler crosses midcourt, X1 and X4 put on the trap. X3 cuts any pass to the middle, X5 protects on the ball side of the lane, and X2 prevents a pass to the left corner.

Pressing Zone Defenses

The normal zone defense picks up the opponent just outside the top of the circle. However, as in the man-for-man defense, the position of pickup can vary from mid-court to three-quarter to full court.

The most common pressing zone defenses are:

1. The 1–3–1 half-court zone press (fig. 6.14)
2. The 1–2–1–1 full court zone press (fig. 6.15)
3. The 2–2–1 full court zone press (fig. 6.16)

As with man-for-man presses, these zone presses are used against poor ball-handling teams, a methodical-pattern-type team in an effort to speed up play, and when the defensive team is trailing late in the game.

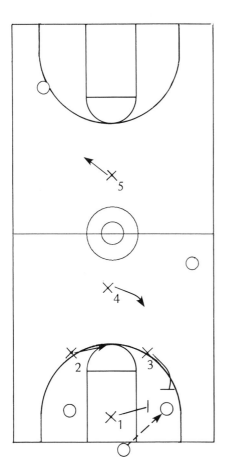

Figure 6.15
The 1-2-1-1 full-court zone press. On the throw-in, X1 and X3 trap the ball while X4 prevents a pass to the midcourt area, and X2 protects the middle of the court.

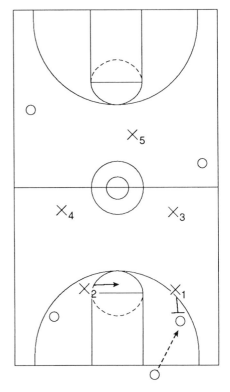

Figure 6.16
The 2-2-1 full-court zone press. On the throw-in, X1 moves to put pressure on the pass receiver as X2 moves to protect the middle of the court. The double-team is usually not applied in this type of press except near the midcourt line.

The basic move of the zone press sends two players onto the ball in what is termed a *trap*. This leaves an offensive player open somewhere on the court. Therefore, a good pass by the offense can result in having the defense outnumbered similar to a fast-break situation. Once this good pass is made it is tremendously important that the defense chase the ball at full speed. This chase of the ball is referred to by coaches as *pursuit*. Many feel that good pursuit of the ball is the real key to a successful zone press.

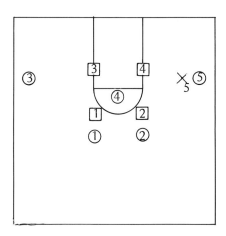 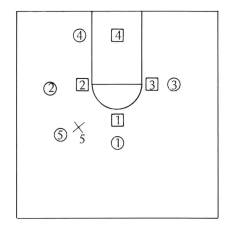

Figure 6.17
Box-and-one combination defense.
Defensive players 1, 2, 3, and 4 set up a
four-player zone defense while defensive
player X5 guards the opposing star man-for-
man.

Figure 6.18
Diamond-and-one combination defense.
Defensive players 1, 2, 3, and 4 set up a
four-player-diamond zone defense while
defensive player X5 guards the opposing
star man-for-man.

Combination Defenses

A variety of combination defenses have been used by coaches to combat particular strengths or to take advantage of weaknesses in the offense of opponents.
The most popular of these defenses are the four-player zone—one-player man-
for-man, and the three-player zone—two-player man-for-man. These defenses
are effective when the offense has one or two real scoring threats, with their teammates being weak scorers.

Four-Player Zone—One-Player Man-for-Man

In this defense, four defenders play zone and one defensive player is assigned the
opposing high scorer. It is used primarily against the so-called "one-player teams"
and is an excellent method for defensing the opposing star.

Two methods are commonly used in playing this defense:

1. Box-and-one (fig. 6.17)
2. Diamond-and-one (fig. 6.18)

The "box-and-one" is stronger at the guard position and weaker at forward,
while the "diamond-and-one" is stronger at the forward position and weaker at
the guards and in the corners. The position played by the opposing star that will
be defensed man-for-man will determine which of the two defenses should be
used. If the opposing star is a guard, strength will not be needed at the guard
position since the one player playing man-for-man will be defensing the star at

that position. Consequently, the diamond-and-one should be selected. However, if the opposing star is a forward, more strength will be needed in the guard defensive area; therefore the box-and-one is more likely to prove successful.

If the star of the opposing team is a forward, which method would you choose in playing the four-player zone—one-player man-for-man defense and why?

Three-Player Zone—Two-Player Man-for-Man

This defense is an excellent one for the team that has two top threats, so often encountered in amateur basketball. Three defenders play in triangular zone positions and two defensive players are assigned to the two-top-scoring opponents. Figure 6.19 diagrams this defense. The zone shifts are similar to those made by rear-line defenders of the 2–1–2 zone defense.

One Defense or Several?

With the different positions of pickup and various defensive maneuvers, it can be seen that quite a number of defenses are available to the basketball coach. An interesting problem faces the astute observer of the game. Is it better for a team to play one defense and spend its practice time mastering this defense so the players will know all of the maneuvers and shifts necessary to make it successful? Or should a team play several defenses, realizing that it will not be able to perfect one particular defense as well, but expecting to gain the advantage of various strengths and weaknesses of particular opponents? Opinion varies on this question, though there are probably more coaches who adhere to the latter philosophy than the former.

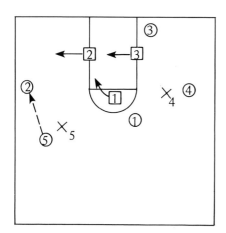

Figure 6.19
The three-player-triangle zone—two-player man-for-man combination defense. Defensive players 1, 2, and 3 play zone defense, and defensive players X4 and X5 guard the two best opponents man-for-man. Shifting responsibilities are shown on the pass from X5 to X2.

The Strategy of the Game

7

As in all games, strategy is important to both the individual player and the team. On numerous occasions, a team with inferior personnel has been able to defeat an opponent simply by the timely use of clever strategy. Since basketball has become a game of varied offenses and defenses, it is imperative that a basketball team be made up of players who have the ability to think in pressure situations.

Individual Strategy

The most important thing you should do strategically as an individual is to analyze your particular opponent. How good is the opponent offensively and why? Can the opponent shoot well from outside? If not, then you should play loosely. Can the opponent drive both ways? If not, then overplay to the side the opponent prefers to drive. (This is a major weakness of most beginning players, so be alert for this strategy.) How does your opponent move without the ball? If not well, then play tightly and your opponent will have a difficult time getting the ball. The player certainly cannot score without ball possession. Determine your opponent's speed. If fast, play looser than normal. What about ball handling? If your opponent is a poor ball handler, press tightly, attempting to force mistakes.

Defensively, if your opponent is playing you loosely, be ready to take the outside shot. Is your opponent a "head turner?" If so, then be ready to cut for a pass and score. If you are being overplayed, be ready to cut backdoor to receive a pass. If you are being defensed tightly, be prepared to drive or screen for a teammate. Watch your opponent's feet and drive to the side of the advanced foot. For example, if the right foot is forward, drive to your opponent's right since that side will be more difficult for your opponent to cover.

Team Strategy

Your team should use the following strategy to begin a game. You must determine what type of offense and what type of defense your opponents are playing, then use the correct offense and defense to combat each. Are your opponents playing a zone defense or are they playing man-for-man? You can determine this by sending cutters through your opponent's defense. If they do not go with the cutters, then you know they are playing a zone defense. Are they playing a single-pose offense, a double-post offense, or another offense? If they are playing a double-post, make certain your best post defenders are guarding their post players. Are your opponents using a fast break? If they are, make certain you have at least two defensive players back to stop their break.

It is vitally important to analyze your particular opponent's offensive play. What might you note that signals you to guard tightly?

Analyze the opposing players as a team just as thoroughly as you would analyze your individual opponent. Know the weaker defensive players and attack their areas. If the team has a particularly strong rebounder, try to pull that rebounder away from the basket by letting the rebounder's assigned opponent play outside. If this is a poor-ball-handling team, an inexperienced team, or a methodical pattern-type team, be ready to use a full court pressing defense.

Playing for One

A fine tool is the strategy of "playing for one." This term simply means that a team plays for one last shot prior to the end of the period. The theory is to take the shot so near the end of the period that the opponent will not have an opportunity to rebound any missed attempt and go downcourt and score. When using this strategy, most teams try to keep the ball until five to eight seconds remain in the period; then a shot is taken. This provides ample time for a chance at an offensive rebound if the shot attempt is missed. It does not, however, leave enough time for the opponent to rebound the ball and take it downcourt into scoring position. Playing for one can often mean the difference between victory and defeat in a close contest. It is a particularly useful strategy for teams that play quarters and have four different periods during the game.

If your opponents are playing for one, you can switch to a more aggressive defense. Since they do not want to shoot until less than ten seconds remain in the period, any defensive mistake you make prior to that time will probably not be exploited by the offense. Therefore, you can gamble for interceptions and any resulting steal might turn into an easy score.

When to Press

An important part of game strategy is knowing when to press or when to use any of the pressing defenses that are available. Generally, pressing defenses are used when a team is trailing late in the game. Quick ball possession is a must, and you cannot allow the opponent to consume time by bringing the ball downcourt slowly. You must challenge the ball downcourt in an effort to steal a pass or force a mistake. Sometimes a team will make the mistake of waiting too late to employ the press. Teams trailing by ten points have been known to wait until three minutes to go to begin the press, find themselves defeated by two points, and then say "If we'd had just one minute more" or "If we had just started to press earlier." It is far better to begin to press too early than to wait until it is too late.

There are other reasons to press in addition to that of making an effort to come from behind. Pressing defenses are good surprise elements. They are particularly effective against an inexperienced opponent, a weak-ball-handling team, a poorly conditioned team, and teams that rely heavily on set plays. If an opponent is trying to slow down the game against a fast-breaking team, the latter must have the ability to go out and harass the opposition in an effort to speed up their play.

The type of press you use will depend on both your personnel and that of your opponent. If your team is a small, quick team, you may find a man-for-man press is best. If your teammates are taller but slow, a type of zone press will probably be more effective. If your opposing guards are mediocre dribblers, a good man-for-man press can force mistakes. On the other hand, if your opponents have an excellent dribbler who is getting the ball upcourt constantly, you will need to zone press and apply double-team tactics on that dribbler.

If a freeze is to be attempted it is often wise to make substitutions. Which of these abilities are particularly important to the success of a freeze: rebounding, free throw, ball handling, shooting field goals?

When to Freeze

Another important part of game strategy is the use of the freeze or stall offense—controlling the ball late in the game when leading by a few points. Various offenses have been devised to enable a team to freeze the basketball. Many teams simply run their own basic formation and refuse to take any shots other than a lay-up shot.

Of course, teams that play with a shot clock can stall only for the duration of the clock. College men use the forty-five-second clock, while college women use the thirty-second clock. Because of this, the stall or freeze in college basketball has been curtailed. High-school and other teams that play without a shot clock must plan to use a stall or freeze offense for late-game situations.

It is rather difficult to establish an ironclad rule to determine when to begin a freeze, since the size of the lead will determine the time. If a team has a five- or six-point lead, its members will have a good chance of freezing the ball for two or three minutes. If the lead is only two or three points, however, three minutes is quite a long time to freeze. On the other hand, the freeze is certainly in order with a two-point lead with one minute to go.

Regardless of the time a team employs the freeze, certain rules should be observed. The better ball handlers should do the majority of the ball handling. These same players should be good free throw shooters, because the defense often fouls and the freeze is of no avail if the free throw is missed. The offense should be spread regardless of formation, and screens on the ball should be avoided to prevent any opportunities by the defense to use double-teaming tactics. It is wise strategy to give the ball to an offensive player who is being guarded by a slow opponent. For example, pulling the offensive center away from the basket and giving the center the ball is usually a sound maneuver, since the defensive center

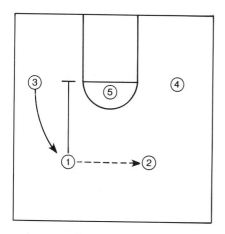

Figure 7.1
A typical freeze pattern. O1 passes to O2 and screens for O3. Notice that all the players are above the free-throw line, which opens up the basket area for cuts to the basket when the defense overplays.

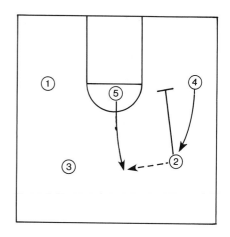

Figure 7.2
If O2 cannot pass to O3, O5 pops out to receive the ball. O2 will pass and then screen for O4.

is normally the weakest player at outside pressing defense. To employ this latter strategy, however, the offensive center must be a capable ball handler and a good free throw shooter.

The freeze can be so important to a team that it is wise to make substitutions at this point in order to remove the weaker ball handlers even though they may be good scorers and rebounders. At this stage of the game, possession of the ball is of paramount importance, and a mistake by a poor ball handler can prove fatal.

The Use of Time-Outs

Time-outs are very important to the success of a basketball team. Five time-outs are allowed during the regulation game, plus one additional time-out for each overtime period. The time-out may be used to stop a particular rally or hot streak by the opponent. Another important reason for a time-out is to change your team's offensive or defensive strategy, or to prepare for a change in the offensive or defensive strategy of the opponent. It is rather difficult to change the strategy without a time-out, for all players must be aware of the change. The time-out also is useful as a rest period, particularly late in a period.

Time-outs are of particular value during the last few minutes of play in a close game. It is during this time that various strategies and special plays usually are employed and quite a few changes made. It therefore is wise to save at least two of a team's five time-outs until the last few minutes of play.

Strategy for the Three-Point Shot

Offensive Strategy

A team must make a number of offensive decisions regarding the three-point shot. First of all, who will take the shot and when? Obviously, only the better three-point shooters on a team should take the shot from this range. Some players may be good enough to take the shot at virtually any time, while others should shoot only when open and with plenty of time. Therefore, when the shot will be taken will vary with the quality of the shooter and the stage of the game.

Many decisions regarding when to shoot the three-point shot will come during the last minutes of a game. Obviously, when a team is trailing by three points with five seconds left on the clock, the best strategy will be to go for the three-point shot to tie the game. However, there are other situations that are less certain. For example, your team trails by three points with thirty seconds left in the game. Do you go for the three-point shot immediately, or do you go for the two and hope to gain possession for another two-point attempt?

Following are other late-game situations and suggested strategies regarding the three-point shot:

1. *Down 5 with 50 seconds to go.* Take what the defense gives you. You must have two possessions and it will not matter a great deal whether you get the three-pointer on the first or second possession.
2. *Down 2 with 10 seconds to go.* If the strength of your team is inside, go for the two-pointer to tie. If your inside play is not good and you have a quality three-point shooter, go for three and the win. The added advantage of going inside for the two-pointer is that you have a better chance of getting fouled on an inside shot. If you do get fouled on a made inside shot, the free throw can win the game. If you are fouled on a missed attempt, you still have the two-shot opportunity at the line.
3. *Down 3 with 30 seconds to go.* This is a tough decision. You can go for three to tie immediately, or go inside for two, then press to attempt to gain possession. Another possession could result in a two-point score and the win. What you do could depend on how good a ball-handling team you are facing. Even when facing a team that handles the ball well, you have the opportunity to foul and gain possession by a missed free throw attempt.
4. *Down 7 with 2 minutes to go.* Go for three! If successful, it will give your team a psychological boost. When you gain possession again, you will trail by only four. Take what the defense gives you, for you still need two possessions.
5. *Down 6 with 1 minute to go.* Go for three! It will take three possessions to tie if you go for two each time, while only two possessions are needed for a tie with successful three-point shots.

Defensive Strategy

The most important part of three-point defensive strategy is to know how many three-point shooters are on the opposing team *and who they are*. The more three-point shooters an opponent has in the lineup, the more defensive problems there will be.

The number of three-point shooters on the opposing team will vary from game to game and will influence the type of defense that can be played. Most teams will have no more than one good three-point shooter, and either a zone or man-for-man defense can be effective if defensive players remain conscious of where the three-point shooter is. Those teams that have two or three three-point shooters pose a different problem. A standard zone defense may not work. Even playing a man-for-man defense may require some adjustment of the normal helpside defensive rules. This is because the offense tends to get more three-point shots by quick reversals of the ball to what was the helpside of the court.

Combination defenses are a good alternative as a defensive strategy for the three-point shot. If a team has one excellent three-point shooter, either the box-and-one or diamond-and-one defense can be strong. However, if a team has two good three-point shooters, a triangle and two may be the best defense.

Defensive Considerations

1. You must determine who the good three-point shooters are on the opposing team.
2. When going against the good three-point shooter, play the shooter tough and force the drive.
3. Guards must be very aware of their importance in defensive rebounding since the ball rebounds farther out.
4. When you foul a three-point shooter, it can be a four-point play!
5. Regardless of the type of defense being used, the defenders must be constantly aware of *who* and *where* the three-point shooters are.
6. Switch on all screens during a last-second attempt by your opponent to get a three-point shot.
7. In all late-game situations, you must know the foul situation. Do you have a foul to give? If so, use a foul to prevent a three-point attempt and buy some time off the clock.

Late-Game Defensive Situations

The following are late-game situations and suggested defensive strategies regarding the three-point shot:

1. *Up 3 with 30 seconds to go.* You must play excellent defense, protecting inside yet covering three-point shooters. You must not foul! Attempt to cover the three-point shooter and prevent a shot that could tie the game. However, the overall defense must be good enough to prevent a quick inside score with

plenty of time left for the opponent to steal the ball for a two-point shot that would win the game. In this situation, the nearer the end of the game, the tighter the defense should be on the three-point shooter.

2. *Up 2 with 30 seconds to go.* This is a very dangerous situation, for a three-point shot can win the game. Most opponents probably will go for two, so the emphasis must be on good basket-protection defense *without fouling.* However, you still must be aware of the location of three-point shooters.

3. *Up 6 with 1 minute to go.* In this situation the opponent will be more interested in a three-point attempt, so the emphasis of your defense must be on protecting against the three-point attempt without fouling. A two-pointer by the opponent will still require them to have two possessions, while a three-pointer will require only one possession for them to have a shot at a tie.

4. *Up 9 with 1 minute to go.* This is a situation where you *know* the opponent is going for three, so play the three-point shooters tightly, force them to drive, and *switch on screens.*

5. *Up 5 with 40 seconds to go.* This is an interesting situation because the opponent can elect to go for either two or three. They may go for an immediate three so they will trail by only two, or they may go for the higher-percentage two so they will be within range with a three-pointer. Some teams may elect to go for three, trail by two if successful, then go for three to win. Therefore, this situation requires more emphasis on preventing the three-point shot.

6. *Up 3 with 15 seconds to go—your team has a foul to give.* In this situation you would like to make a foul prior to any shot attempt, since your opponent will not get a free throw but instead will have to take the ball out-of-bounds. Your objective will be to make your opponent use up as much of the fifteen seconds as possible without allowing them a shot.

Origin and Development of Basketball

8

Basketball is one of the few sports that had its start in the United States. It is truly an American game and its popularity in this country has been amazing. It was invented at Springfield College in 1891 by Dr. James Naismith, a physical education instructor who sought to develop a game for Springfield men to satisfy their desire for physical activity between the football and baseball seasons. Peach baskets were used as the first goals and a soccer ball served as the first ball. When a team scored it was necessary to bring out a ladder; some player then would climb up to remove the ball from the basket. Finally, the bottom of the peach basket was removed so that play could be speeded up. First rules were simple and the number of players allowed on each team depended on the size of the gymnasium.

Basketball was well received by participants from the beginning, and it was not long before colleges and YMCAs began forming teams. Yale fielded a team in 1892. Cornell and the University of Chicago had teams a year later.[1] Yale and Pennsylvania played the first intercollegiate basketball game in 1897.[2] After the turn of the century, the game enjoyed amazing growth. It spread rapidly from the colleges and YMCAs to the junior and senior high schools and playgrounds throughout the country, until today it is played by men and women in every village and hamlet throughout the United States and in virtually every nation.

Significant Rule Changes

A considerable number of changes and additions to Dr. Naismith's thirteen original rules have been made over the years. Perhaps the most significant single rule change was the elimination of the center jump in the early 1930s. The original game required a jump ball at center court each time a team scored. This resulted in slow play, low-scoring games, and not too much spectator interest.

Which current rules were designed to lessen the edge afforded by superior height? Which rules change voted in 1976 gave back to tall players an advantage they had temporarily lost? Do you think this rule change was justified?

The time-limitation rules have also greatly influenced the game. The first, the "ten-second rule," requires the ball to be advanced into front court within ten seconds. This prevents teams from withholding the ball from play at full-court distance away from their basket. All boys' and men's teams and most high-school girls' teams in the nation play this rule; however, women's collegiate teams and some high-school girls' teams have adopted the "thirty-second clock," requiring a shot within thirty seconds of possession. Therefore, these teams have eliminated the ten-second rule.

The second significant rule change in basketball, known as the "three-second" rule, prevents offensive players from remaining within the offensive free throw lane for more than three seconds. This rule was passed in an effort to reduce the effectiveness of the tall player.

The "bonus" free throw rule was added in 1954. This rule gives the player who is fouled while not in the act of shooting a second or bonus free throw if the first free throw is successful. This led to what some critics have referred to as "a parade to the free throw line," so the rule has now been altered—it does not go into effect until the seventh foul in each half in college basketball, and the fifth foul in high-school basketball.

Another change designed to curb the effectiveness of the tall player was legislated in 1957. At that time the free throw lane was widened from six to twelve feet. Since no offensive player can remain in this lane area more than three seconds, this forces taller players away from the basket and requires them to develop more offensive maneuverability. It also helps open up the middle area for drives. It would not be surprising to see the lane widened even more in the future.

The Most Significant Rule Change for Women

A most significant change in the rules for women's basketball occurred in 1971 with the adoption of five-on-five basketball for girls and women.[3] Prior to the change, women's basketball was played with three forwards and three guards. The forwards were on one side of the center line and the guards on the other side. Neither could cross the center line. This made the game a "half-court" game for the players. Now, colleges and all but two state high-school associations have adopted the five-on-five full court game as in men's basketball.

The Three-Point Shot

In the spring of 1986 the college rules committee added the three-point field goal to college basketball, and the following year the National Federation of High School Athletic Associations followed suit. The rule change probably will have as much effect on the game of basketball as any other rule change in history. It is the first time since the inception of basketball that an extra point has been given for a field goal from long range. It will require changes in offensive and defensive strategy and will add excitement to the game, particularly in the late minutes.

Both the colllege and high-school rules committees established the distance for the three-point shot at 19'9". Considerable argument ensued concerning the distance. Many coaches and fans felt the distance was too short and expected it to be increased for the following season; however, this did not occur and it is doubtful that the distance will be changed in the near future.

It is amazing how much excitement the three-point shot has added to the game. The most exciting feature of the shot is that it allows the trailing team to make up a larger deficit than the two-point shot allowed. Prior to the three-point shot, a ten-point lead with two minutes to go in a game was considered virtually a guarantee of victory. Now, a trailing team in this situation is no longer "out of the game." Instead of five possessions needed for a tie, four possessions gain the tie. Since the adoption of the rule, numerous games have been won with the three-pointer in the last minutes of play, with fans and coaches kept on the edge of their seats even until the last seconds of games.

The Jump Shot

Probably the most significant fundamental development in basketball has been the development of the jump shot, which has ocurred during the past thirty years. Prior to 1950, all one-handed shooting was done with at least one foot on the playing court. It was discovered, however, that players could still achieve accuracy by shooting fom the top of their jump, thus making it far more difficult for the defense to block, and more and more players began using the jump shot. As college and professional players became proficient with the jump shot, high-school players copied the technique and it has now become the most often-used shot in the game.

"Dunking"

When Lew Alcindor, now known as Kareem Jabbar, enrolled at UCLA, rules-makers made it illegal to "dunk" the basketball. However, the rules committee voted in 1976 to legalize the dunk again beginning with the 1976–77 season. Since then, this crowd-pleasing shot has played a significant part in many college teams' offenses. One drawback to the dunk is that it has caused the glass backboard to shatter on occasion, causing long delays or postponement of games. Because of this danger of damage to the backboard, dunking is not allowed during warm-up but only in actual game play.

Gymnasium Development

Early gymnasiums were moderate in size, had limited seating capacity, and the playing courts were smaller than the regulation floors of today. However, as rule changes increased the speed of play, and the skill of the individual players improved, the popularity of the game increased. This brought about the need for larger facilities to accommodate the ever-growing number of spectators, a growth which has become increasingly apparent throughout the country. Today many colleges have gymnasiums seating from ten to fifteen thousand, and it is not uncommon for a high-school gymnasium to seat four or five thousand. The University of Tennessee's new gymnasium seats 25,000 spectators, and the University of Kentucky's Rupp Arena seats 23,000 spectators and is sold out for each season. Though not gymnasiums, the Superdome in New Orleans, the Astrodome in Houston, the Kingdome in Seattle, and the Silverdome in Detroit are used for basketball and draw large crowds for NCAA tournaments and key professional games. More than 60,000 spectators witnessed Indiana University defeat Syracuse for the NCAA national championship in the Superdome in 1986.

The Four Most Famous Teams

The four most famous teams in basketball were the Original Celtics, the Boston Celtics, the Los Angeles Lakers, and the Harlem Globetrotters. The Original Celtics were organized in 1914 and toured the United States for seven years, amassing an amazing record of 1,320 wins against only 66 losses. They were so strong that when they joined the American professional league they were broken up to give the other teams balance.[4]

The Boston Celtics of the National Basketball Association have dominated the game more than any other team in sports history. Coached by the "winningest coach in basketball," Arnold "Red" Auerbach, the Celtics won eight consecutive NBA titles and nine championships in ten years.

In 1988 the Los Angeles Lakers became the first team to win back-to-back NBA championships in nineteen years. Coached by Pat Riley and led by "Magic" Johnson and James Worthy, the Lakers defeated the Detroit Pistons in a seven-game series for the 1988 title.

Without any question whatsoever, the Harlem Globetrotters are the most colorful team in basketball. Organized by Abe Saperstein, the Globetrotters have combined fantastic skill with ingenious comedy to become the most well-known basketball team. They play annually before packed houses throughout the world and have done more than any other team to popularize basketball internationally.

Language of the Game

Assist—A pass that results in a score.

Backboard—The rectangular or fan-shaped board behind the goal that often is used for banking shots.

Backcourt—The half of the court that is farthest from the offensive basket.

Backdoor—A cut along the baseline when a player is being overplayed by the defense or when the defense turns to look at the ball.

Ballside—The side of the defensive court in which possession of the ball is located.

Baseball Pass—A pass thrown with the same basic technique that is used when throwing a baseball, and usually employed for long downcourt passes.

Baseline—The end line running under the basket from sideline to sideline.

Basket—The goal.

Blocking Off the Boards—The positioning of a defensive player in such a manner as to prevent an offensive player from going to the basket for a rebound. Also referred to as "box out" or "block out."

Bounce Pass—A pass that strikes the floor before it gets to the receiver.

Box-and-One—A combination defense in which four players play zone and one player plays man-for-man.

Carrying—Same as traveling.

Center—A position usually played by the tallest player on the team.

Change of Pace—An offensive technique, usually used by the dribbler, in which speed is reduced then quickly increased to evade a defender.

Charging—Running into a player who is stationary.

Chest Pass—A two-hand pass that is begun from the passer's chest and pushed toward the receiver so it can be received in that same vicinity.

Clear Out—An offensive technique in which a player close to a teammate with the ball cuts away from that teammate so that his or her defensive opponent cannot help out on any drive attempt.

Controlling the Boards—Gaining a majority of the rebounds.

Cut—A quick move by an offensive player, usually toward his or her basket.

Defensive Rebounding—Rebounding at the opponent's end of the court.

Diamond-and-One—Similar to box-and-one except four of the defensive players line up in a diamond formation in relation to the basket.

Double Dribble—Player continuing to dribble after touching the ball with both hands.

Double Pivot—A type of team offense in which two players play in the pivot area.

Double Screen—A screen set by two players.

Double Team—A defensive tactic of using two players to guard the player with the ball.

Drive—A quick dribble toward the basket in an effort to score.

Dunking—Slamming the ball down through the goal. Also called "stuffing."

Fast Break—A situation in which the defensive team gains possession of the ball and moves into scoring position so quickly that its members outnumber the opponents downcourt.

Filling the Lanes—Cutting players into the three hypothetical lanes necessary for a three-on-two break situation.

Flex Offense—A continuity-type offense in which players learn to play all five positions.

Flip Pass—A pass made with one hand when exchanging the ball at close range.

Forward—A position usually played by one of the taller players, requiring both shooting and rebounding ability. The forward usually plays close to the sideline and toward the corner near the offensive basket.

Free Throw—An unguarded shot from the free-throw line that is the result of a foul by the opponent.

Freezing the Ball—Keeping the ball in play without any effort to score, a tactic often used late in a game in an effort to protect a slight lead.

Fronting the Post—Guarding the pivot player in front rather than between that player and the basket. It is a defensive tactic necessary to keep a good pivot player from obtaining possession of the ball close to the basket.

Give and Go—Passing the ball to a teammate and cutting hard to the basket for a return pass.

Goaltending—Touching the ball or basket when the ball is above, on, or within either basket.

Guard—A position usually played by the smaller players. It requires good ball handling and passing as well as the ability to shoot from the outside.

Helpside—The side of the defensive court in which no player has possession of the ball.

High Post—An offensive player who plays near the free-throw line.

Hook Pass—A pass thrown with one hand in a sweeping motion over the head.

Hook Shot—A shot taken with one hand in a sweeping motion over the head. It usually is taken close to the basket.

Hoop—The basket, or goal.

Jump Ball—The situation involving joint possession, in which the official tosses the ball into the air and two opposing players jump in an effort to tap it toward a teammate—also referred to as a "toss-up."

Jump Shot—A shot taken after the shooter has jumped into the air.

Key—The area close to the basket that includes the free-throw lane.

Lay-up Shot—A shot taken close to the basket, usually with one hand.

Low Post—An offensive player who plays near the basket with his or her back to the basket.

Man-for-Man—A team defense in which players are assigned specific opponents to guard wherever those opponents may go in the offensive pattern.

Offensive Rebounding—Rebounding at the offensive end of the floor.

One-on-One—The situation in which one offensive player tries to score against one defensive player.

Outlet Pass—A pass made after a defensive rebound.

Overtime—An extra period played to break a tie score.

Palming—When the dribbler's hand is placed under the ball and then the dribble continued. Same as a traveling violation.

Pass—A ball thrown from one player to another.

Pass and Cut—An offensive maneuver in which a player passes to a teammate and cuts to the basket for a return pass. It is often called "give and go."

Passing Game—A type of offense, often referred to as "motion," in which players move in a free-lance manner but under a set of rules.

Peripheral Vision—Also referred to as "split vision." The ability to see to the side while looking ahead.

Pick—Same as a screen.

Pivot—Footwork that enables the ball handler to move one foot while keeping the other in the same position of contact on the floor. Also, a position on the court near the basket where the tallest player usually is stationed.

Pivot Area—The area close to the basket where the center generally plays.

Pivot Player—A player who plays close to the basket.

Playing for One—The strategy of playing for one shot just prior to the end of a period.

Post—A pivot player stationed near the basket and facing away from it.

Can you speak the language? Check your understanding of these terms: sagging defense, split the post, screen and roll, trailer.

Press Defense—A forcing-type defense in which the offense is picked up farther away from the basket than normal. The press may be a half-court, three-quarter-court, or full court type.

Rebound—A missed shot attempt.

Reverse Dribble—The dribble technique in which the dribbler changes direction by making a complete turn so that the body will protect the ball as the dribble is continued.

Running—Same as traveling.

Sagging Defense—A defense that drops back toward the free-throw lane to jam the area close to the basket. It is very effective when playing against a strong pivot player.

Screen—A maneuver used by the offense in an effort to free a player for a shot at the basket. The screener stands in such a position that the opposing defensive player cannot get to the player who is in position to shoot.

Screen and Roll—An offensive technique in which the screener pivots on the inside foot and cuts to the basket. The technique is used to combat a switching defense.

Second Guard—A very pouplar play in which one guard passes to a forward and then cuts through, and the forward hands off to the second guard coming around.

Set Shot—A shot taken from long range and a stationary position.

Single Pivot—A type of team offense in which one player plays in the pivot area.

Split-the-Post—A three-player offensive maneuver in which the ball is passed to a post player and two players then scissor off this post player for a possible pass.

Stall—An offensive technique in which a team makes little effort to score. It usually is used by a team late in the game in an effort to kill the clock. Similar to the freeze.

Stuffing—Same as dunking.

Switch—A maneuver used by the defense to combat a screen and make possible a change of defensive assignments.

Switch Dribble—A technique in which the dribbler changes dribbling hands by crossing the ball in front of the body.

Ten-Second Line—The midcourt line over which the team possessing the ball must advance within ten seconds.

Three-on-Two—A fast break situation in which three offensive players attack two defensive players.

Three-Point Shot—A shot taken from a distance of at least 19'9" from the basket and that counts three points.

Three-Second Lane—The offensive free throw lane in which no offensive player can remain for more than three seconds at a time.

Tip-in—A quick one-handed tip of a missed field-goal try that results in a score.

Trailer—An offensive player who comes downcourt after his or her teammates have tried to score on a three-on-two situation. The trailer can be available for an outlet pass for a quick shot or to cut through for a lay-up or rebound.

Traveling—Taking more than one step with the ball without dribbling. Also referred to as "walking."

Triple-Threat Position—Holding the ball near the hip in such a manner that the player can shoot, drive, or pass.

Turnover—Any loss of ball possession caused by a violation.

Two-on-One—A fast break situation in which two offensive players attempt to score on one defensive player.

Violation—A rules violation that results in loss of the ball.

Weave—A type of offense involving close exchanges of the ball. The weave may be a three-player, four-player, or five-player type.

Zone Defense—A team defense in which a defensive player is assigned an area on the court to guard.

Notes

1. Forrest Anderson and Stan Allbeck, *Coaching Better Basketball* (New York: The Ronald Press Company, 1964), 5.
2. Ibid.
3. Frances H. Ebert and Billye Ann Cheatum, *Basketball,* 2nd ed. (W. B. Saunders Co., 1977), 12.
4. John Durant and Otto Bettman, *Pictorial History of American Sports* (New York: A. S. Barnes Co., 1952), 166.

Rules of The Game

9

Basketball rules in the United States are rather standardized for all levels of play. There are only a few exceptions. The major differences involve the size of the playing court and the length of playing periods; both become slightly longer as the age and skill of players increase. Rule books are published annually by the National Collegiate Athletic Association, by state high-school athletic associations, and by the National Association for Girls and Women in Sport. The following resume of the rules will suffice for normal recreational play.

Playing Court, Goal, and Ball

The recommended size of the playing court is as follows: college and professional, 50' × 94'; high school, 50' × 84'. Refer to figure 9.1 for complete dimensions of the playing court. Notice that the free throw lane is twelve feet in width.

The backboards to which the goals are attached are constructed of any rigid material. They shall be either of two types: (1) a rectangle 6' wide by 4' high, or (2) fan-shaped—54" wide by 35" high.

Each basket must be attached to the backboard parallel to the floor. The inside diameter of the basket is eighteen inches, and the basket is placed ten feet above the playing floor.

The ball must be spherical, but its size varies for men and women. The men's ball must have a circumference of between 29½ and 30 inches with a weight of not less than twenty nor more than twenty-two ounces. The women's ball must have a circumference of between 28½ and 29 inches with a weight of not less than eighteen ounces nor more than twenty ounces.

Players and Substitutes

Each team consists of five players plus substitutes. Each team designates a captain who represents the team and may confer with officials on questions regarding interpretation of the rules or other basic information. Such discussion must be done in a courteous manner.

When substitutes desire to enter the game, they must give their names and numbers to the official scorer. They may enter when they are beckoned by the official after the scorer has sounded the horn when the ball is dead and time is out.

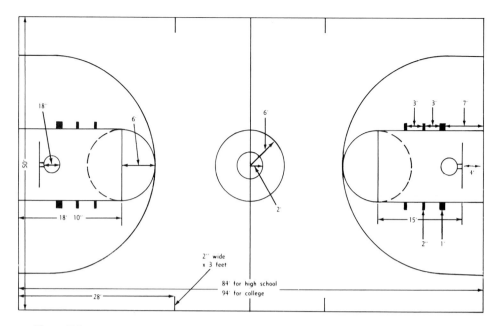

Figure 9.1
Dimensions of a basketball court. All lines should be two inches in width.

A number must be worn on both the front and back of a player's jersey. The number on the back must be at least six inches high and that on the front at least four inches high. The single digit numbers 1 and 2 or any digit greater than 5 cannot be used. For example, the number 26 is illegal since one of the digits is greater than 5. The wearing of an illegal number results in the charge of a technical foul against the captain of the team.

Scoring and Timing

A field goal is scored when a live ball enters the basket from above and passes down through it. Such a goal scored from a distance of at least 19'9" counts three points, and all others from closer range count two points. When a free throw is awarded for a foul, each successful free throw counts one point. If a player mistakenly shoots a field goal into the opponent's basket, the goal is counted for the opponent.

The length of the game shall be as follows:

1. College: Two halves of twenty minutes each with a fifteen-minute intermission between halves.
2. High school: Four quarters of eight minutes each with a ten-minute intermission between halves and a one-minute intermission after the first and third quarters.

3. Below high school: Four quarters of six minutes each with the same intermission as for high schools.
4. The professional game is played in four twelve-minute quarters.

Each period ends when time expires, but a shot in flight when time expires counts as a score even if made after the period ends.

If the score is tied at the end of the regulation game, one or more overtime periods are played until a winner is determined. College overtime periods are five minutes in length and high-school extra periods are three minutes in length. Teams change baskets at the beginning of the first extra period but do not change again regardless of the number of extra periods which must be played.

Each team is allowed five charged time-outs during the game. For each overtime period, an additional time-out is granted each team. A technical foul is charged for each additional time-out.

A game is started by a jump ball that is taken by two opponents at the center line. After the ball is put in play, play continues and the clock runs until a violation occurs, the ball goes out of bounds, a personal foul occurs, or a time-out is called.

Both men and women in college basketball use a shot clock to avoid excessive stalling tactics. College men use a forty-five-second clock, while college women use a thirty-second clock. A few state high school associations require their girls' teams to use the thirty-second clock.

Specific Rule Definitions

The *basket* is the eighteen-inch ring, and its flanges, braces, and net.

Blocking is personal contact which impedes the progress of an opponent who does not have the ball.

A *player* is in control when holding a live ball or dribbling it.

A *team* is in control when a player of the team has the ball, and also while a live ball is being passed between teammates.

A *dribble* is ball movement by a player who taps the ball in the air or on the floor, then touches it once or several times or catches it. Such a dribble ends when the dribbler touches the ball with both hands simultaneously, permits it to come to rest while in contact with it, or loses control of it.

An *air-dribble* is that part of a dribble during which the dribbler throws or taps the ball in the air and then touches it before it touches the floor.

A *foul* is an infraction of the rules, for which one or more free throws are awarded, or ball possession is lost if it is a player-control foul.

A *double foul* is a situation in which two opponents commit personal fouls against each other at approximately the same time.

A *multiple foul* is a situation in which teammates commit a personal foul against the same opponent at approximately the same time.

A *personal foul* results when contact is made with an opponent while the ball is alive.

A *player-control foul* is a personal foul committed by a player while that player's team is in possession of the ball.

A *technical foul* is a foul by either a player or non-player which does not involve contact, or which may involve unsportsmanlike contact with an opponent while the ball is dead. A technical foul also is awarded for other unsportsmanlike acts.

A *free throw* is awarded when a player is fouled or a technical foul is called.

A team's *front court* is that half of the playing court nearest its own basket.

A team's *backcourt* is that half of the playing court nearest its opponent's basket.

Closely guarded is defined as within six feet.

Holding is personal contact with an opponent which prevents the opponent's freedom of movement.

A *jump ball* results when two opposing players gain joint possession of the ball. The ball is tossed by an official into the air between the two players; they jump and attempt to tap it to teammates. Rules for college men were changed at the beginning of the 1981–82 season to eliminate the jump ball except to begin the game and to begin an overtime period.

A *pivot* occurs when a player in possession of the ball steps one or more times in any direction while keeping one foot in contact with the floor. The foot in contact with the floor is called the pivot foot. If a player moves this pivot foot while in possession of the ball, that player is guilty of traveling or running with the ball.

Violations and Penalties

It is a violation to:

1. Dribble again after a player's first dribble is ended.
2. Remain for more than three seconds in the free throw lane on the offensive end of the court while a player or team has possession of the ball.
3. Fail to advance the ball across the midcourt line within ten seconds, unless rules require a thirty-second shot clock.
4. Cause the ball to go backcourt after advancing it across the midcourt line. Again, this does not apply when the thirty-second shot clock is used.
5. Touch the basket or the ball while the ball is on or immediately above the goal.
6. Move into the circle before a jump ball is touched by one of the jumpers.
7. Step into the free throw lane before a free-throw attempt leaves the shooter's hands.
8. Leave the designated throw-in spot when throwing the ball in from out of bounds, and not throwing the ball in within five seconds.
9. Run with the ball.
10. Kick the ball or strike it with the fist.

A personal foul is called if:

1. A player holds, pushes, charges, or trips an opponent.
2. A dribbler charges into an opponent or dribbles between two opponents, unless enough space is provided to enable the dribbler to do so without contact.
3. A player who screens is not stationary and does not take a position at least a normal step away from the opponent.

In general the personal foul is charged to the player who causes bodily contact, whether or not the player is on offense or defense. The penalty is one or more free throws depending upon whether the player was shooting when the foul was committed and how many fouls the player's team has committed in the half. If a player was fouled in the act of shooting, two free throws are awarded unless the try was successful, in which case only one free throw is awarded. If a player is fouled while not in the act of shooting, no free throws are awarded except under the following circumstances:

1. In high school games—the foul is the opponent's fifth during the half, in which case the player is awarded one shot plus a bonus shot if the first shot is successful.
2. In college games—if the foul is the opponent's seventh foul in the half, in which case the player is awarded one shot plus a bonus shot if the first shot is successful. This free-throw situation is referred to as the "one-and-one."

A player is disqualified after committing five personal fouls in a high-school or college game. Professional players are allowed six personal fouls.

A technical foul is awarded for situations such as delaying the game, unsportsmanlike conduct, making illegal substitutions, and using excessive time-outs. The normal penalty for a technical foul is one free throw and ball possession. However, a technical foul on a coach or on the bench results in two free throws and ball possession.

Sportsmanship In Basketball

10

Though no rules are written to cover sportsmanship, it is important for the sake of both safety and enjoyment that players abide by normal rules of sportsmanship.

Players are expected to respect officials and show courtesy to opponents at all times, and to visitors in particular. Many games are played for which one team must travel quite a distance in order to participate. These players will be unfamiliar with the community and facilties. Coaches and players of the home team should be alert to help in any way possible.

Though basketball is sometimes referred to as a noncontact sport, it is far from that; aggressive play with considerable bodily contact is the rule rather than the exception. Many opportunities are present for dirty play; such play may cause serious injury and is likely to result in unusually rough play by both teams. Players who like to pinch the legs of opponents or jab them in the midsection when an official is not looking are a detriment to the game and should not be given the privilege of playing. Avoid dirty play at all times.

You probably will have many opportunities to play the game when no official is present. Good sportsmanship becomes doubly important at these times. Fouls must be called by the players themselves, using the honor system. Out-of-bounds and jump balls also must be called in the same manner, and it is very important that you be entirely honest and fair.

Basketball is a very fast game, and a player's personality can be disclosed rather quickly. You should avoid any display of temper or any emotional outbursts. The player who fails to practice self-control is looked upon with distaste by teammates as well as by opponents and spectators.

Learn to be humble in victory and gracious in defeat. There is no place for the braggart in any game, and poor losers only focus attention on their immaturity.

Remember that basketball is a team game and that team play is of utmost importance. Avoid overshooting. Look for teammates who are in a better position than you are to shoot. Applaud good plays made by your teammates and never blame your teammates for your own failures.

Facts For Enthusiasts

11

National basketball championships, both professional and amateur, are conducted by several national organizations. The National Basketball Association is the premier professional league in the United States, and its annual playoff winner is considered to be the world champion. The National Collegiate Athletic Association has a national champion in three divisions for both men and women. The National Association for Intercollegiate Athletics, primarily made up of many of the nation's small colleges, and the National Junior College Athletic Association have championships for men and women in two divisions. High schools do not compete nationally, but nearly every state holds state championship tournaments for both boys and girls.

It is not uncommon for college basketball teams for men to play before more than 250,000 spectators in a single season; in fact, during the 1986–87 season Syracuse University played before 498,850 spectators at their home games alone. Syracuse plays in the Carrier Dome, where 32,602 spectators saw their game with Georgetown in February of 1987. The largest crowd to see an NCAA basketball game was 64,959 who saw Indiana University defeat Syracuse for the national championship at the Louisiana Superdome in March of 1987.[1]

Many college teams travel more than 25,000 miles in a single season. During the 1979–80 season, Lamar University traveled 43,000 miles, while the University of Cincinnati traveled 40,000 miles.[2]

Pete Maravich of Louisiana State University holds the all-time record for points scored in three years of college play. Maravich, who finished his college career in 1970, scored 3,667 points in three years for an average of 44.2 points per game.[3] Not only does Maravich hold the all-time record for points scored in three seasons, but he also holds the record for career average (44.2 points per game) and the one-season scoring record (1,381 points).[4]

Do you know what percentage of field-goal tries is considered good for a team? What is the record for successful free throws by an individual? How often does the home team win in college basketball?

In 1986–87, Kevin Houston of Army led the nation's major colleges in scoring with 953 points in 29 games for an average of 32.9 points per game. Alan Williams of Princeton led in field-goal percentage, connecting on 163 of 232 field goals attempted for a 70.3 pecentage, while Army's Houston led the nation in free throw percentage with 268 successful free throws in 294 attempts for 91.2 percent. Jerome Lane of Pittsburgh grabbed 444 rebounds, averaging 13.5 per game, tops nationally in that department.[5]

99

The home-court advantage has been a major concern in basketball for many years. One survey indicated the home team came out on top 80 percent of the time in major college basketball.[6]

Several years ago coaches were well satisfied if their teams made 33 percent of their field-goal tries. Today it is difficult to win unless a team shoots better than 40 percent; the nation's team-field-goal-percentage leaders will shoot better than 50 percent. The individual leader shoots better than 60 percent of his or her field goal tries for the season, a percentage Dr. Naismith would find extremely difficult to believe. As a comparison, the Illinois basketball team in 1947–48 finished with a 15–5 record and shot .281 from the field and .565 from the free-throw line.[7]

In 1986–87, Princeton led the nation in team field goal percentage with 601 field goals in 1111 attempts for a 54.1 percentage. The University of Alabama was the team free-throw leader with 521 made free throws in 662 attempts for an average of 78.7 percent.[8]

The all-time leader for points scored in a single college game is Frank Selvy, who scored 100 points in Furman University's win over Newberry in 1954.[9] The most points scored by a college team in a single game was 164 by Nevada–Las Vegas against Hawaii–Hilo in 1976.[10]

Notes

1. *1988 NCAA BASKETBALL* (Mission, Kan.: National Collegiate Athletic Association), 158.
2. *1980 Converse Basketball Yearbook*, 59th ed. (Malden, Mass.: Converse Rubber Co.), 57.
3. *1988 NCAA BASKETBALL*, pp. 19–20.
4. Ibid., pp. 14–20.
5. *Dick Vitale's BASKETBALL* (Seattle, Wash.: Preview Publishing, Inc., 1987), 113.
6. George Solomon, "There's no place like home," *Basketball:* 15.
7. "From Here and There," *Athletic Journal* (April 1966): 14.
8. *Dick Vitale's BASKETBALL*, 113.
9. *1988 NCAA BASKETBALL*, 14.
10. Ibid., 9.

Playing the Game

12

Many opportunities are available for those who would like to play basketball, whether at the beginning, intermediate, or advanced level. One of the distinct advantages of this game over other team sports is that it can be played alone. You can purchase a rubber basketball for approximately fifteen dollars, a goal for slightly more, and construct a backboard with discarded lumber or plywood. A good pair of basketball shoes can be purchased for thirty dollars and you are ready to play. Quite a number of shooting games are available to the individual who wants to shoot alone in the backyard. Most playgrounds throughout the country have basketball goals, and most schools and colleges have gymnasiums that are open daily, thus providing many oportunities for shooting and playing the game.

For the beginner, most opportunities for playing will come on the playground with other novices. It is rather easy to find three or four other players who would like to play two-on-two or three-on-three. Enough players often will be available for five-on-five. When three-on-three is played, usually only one goal is used, while five-on-five usually is played on a full court.

As you improve your play, you may find that you will have the opportunity to play on your school team, either varsity or junior varsity. If you have a desire to play, most coaches will be eager to have you try out for the team, and if you are not good enough for their varsity, they will be pleased to have you play junior-varsity basketball. If your skills are not advanced enough for play on this level, then be sure to participate in the intramural program at your school.

Figure 12.1
A coach gives instructions to her team during a time-out.

If you are not in school, you will find many opportunities in playground leagues, church leagues, or YMCA or YWCA leagues. Check with your local recreation department for full information as to what leagues are available.

Basketball is played year-round, and facilities for the game are improving constantly. If you have a sincere desire to play the game, you will have no trouble finding opportunities. Work at the game daily and play as often as possible and you will be pleasantly surprised at the results you will accomplish.

Questions and Answers

Multiple Choice

1. A distinct advantage of the shuffle offense is that
   a. the middle is kept clear to allow quick cuts to the basket.
   b. players do not have to return to their original positions to continue the offense.
   c. quick cuts and stationary screens enable the offense to get free for numerous set shots.
   d. good ball-handling combined with quick cuts to the basket result in numerous lay-up shots. (p. 51)
2. The box-and-one is used when
   a. the opposing team is a pattern-type team.
   b. the opposing team has one player who is a good shooter.
   c. the opposing team has an unusually high-scoring individual.
   d. the opposing team has an inexperienced player who can be left unguarded. (pp. 73–74)
3. The chief advantage of the hook shot is that
   a. it can be taken quickly.   c. it is difficult to defend.
   b. it can be learned easily.   d. it is very accurate.   (p. 30)
4. The baseball pass is used
   a. to pass to teammates cutting downcourt.
   b. when freezing the ball.
   c. in close exchanges of the ball.
   d. when feeding the cutter off a split-the-post maneuver. (p. 30)
5. A chief disadvantage of the hook pass is that
   a. it cannot be used to pass over a defensive player.
   b. it is difficult to control.
   c. it is difficult to receive.
   d. it usually is thrown too hard. (pp. 30–31)
6. The most common offense known to basketball is the
   a. single-post offense.   c. weave.
   b. double-post offense.   d. tandem-post offense.   (p. 47)
7. The double-post offense is used when
   a. a team has good ball-handlers and desires to control the ball.
   b. a team has excellent shooting guards and desires to set up screens for outside shots.
   c. a team has two tall players they would like to keep close to the basket.
   d. a team has excellent speed and desires to keep the middle open for quick cuts to the basket. (p. 48)

Answer the Following

8. Explain the "triple-threat position." (p. 3)
9. Explain the difference between the speed dribble and the control dribble. (p. 18)
10. What is the primary purpose of the pivot? (p. 20)
11. Which method of free-throw shooting is most pouplar today? Why? (p. 11)
12. What will be the result if a bounce pass strikes the floor too far away from the receiver? (p. 15)
13. What is the key to a successful fast break? (p. 58)
14. Name three types of teams the pressing defense is useful against. (p. 67)
15. What is meant by a "good" shot? (p. 10)
16. In addition to proper shooting mechanics, name three additional factors important in becoming a good free throw shooter. (pp. 11–12)
17. When did the college rules committee add the three-point shot? (p. 60)
18. What is the most important part of defensive strategy for the three-point shot? (p. 80)
19. How should you handle screens on last-second attempts by your opponent to get a three-point shot? (p. 80)

True or False

20. The basket or goal is a cylinder approximately twenty inches in diameter. (p. 1)
21. A free throw from a technical foul scores two points. (p. 1)
22. A free throw from a personal foul scores one point. (p. 1)
23. The ball can be advanced quicker by passing than by dribbling. (p. 1)
24. A team is composed of six players—three guards, two forwards, and a center. (p. 1)
25. In a man-for-man defense, each player has the responsibility of guarding any player in his or her area of the court. (p. 1)
26. A forward needs to excel in ball-handling and dribbling more than in rebounding. (p. 3)
27. The palms of the hand should touch the basketball only when shooting. (p. 3)
28. The lay-up shot should be broad-jumped rather than high-jumped. (p. 5)
29. The jump shot did not become popular until the 1950s. (p. 7)
30. A good jump shooter will practice shooting the jump shot while falling backwards and sideways. (p. 7)
31. When you receive a pass, dribble immediately to prevent defensive pressure. (p. 36)
32. A pivot made on the heel rather than the ball of the foot is a violation. (p. 20)
33. After rebounding a missed shot, it is a foul to move the elbows back and forth even though no contact is made. (p. 21)
34. Proper defensive stance requires the back to be bent. (pp. 23–24)
35. Defensive footwork is similar to that employed by a boxer. (p. 24)
36. Generally, proper defense position requires the defensive player to remain between the opponent and the basket at all times. (pp. 24–26)
37. A good man-for-man defense will prevent the pass into the post area. (p. 65)

38. In a zone defense, each player is assigned a particular area of the floor to defend.
   (p. 68)
39. The hook shot is taken from close range and is begun while facing the basket.
   (p. 29)
40. When throwing the baseball pass, keep the weight on the back foot until after the ball leaves the hand.
   (p. 30)
41. The switch dribble can be made quicker than the reverse dribble.
   (p. 33)
42. Throughout the reverse dribble, the body is kept between the ball and the defensive player.
   (p. 32)
43. The shuffle offense requires all players to play all positions.
   (p. 51)
44. The first option of the shuffle offense is a pass to the forward cutting into the post area.
   (p. 51)
45. The third option of the shuffle offense is a pass to the center at the top of the circle.
   (p. 51)
46. Players dislike the fast break because of the ball handling and conditioning required.
   (p. 58)
47. If your defensive opponent's right foot is forward, drive right since that side will be more difficult for the defender to cover.
   (p. 75)
48. The strategy of "playing for one" should be used early in the game to take advantage of the opponent's weak defensive players.
   (p. 76)
49. Good screens are very important when freezing the ball.
   (p. 77)
50. A team should attempt to save one time-out for the last few minutes of play when strategy is so important.
   (p. 78)
51. Yale was the first college to field a basketball team.
   (p. 83)
52. The bonus-free throw rule goes into effect after the sixth foul in college basketball and after the fourth foul in high-school basketball.
   (p. 84)
53. College teams play two halves of sixteen minutes each with a fifteen-minute half-time intermission.
   (p. 92)
54. A multiple foul is a situation in which two opponents commit personal fouls against each other at approximately the same time.
   (p. 93)
55. It is a violation to touch the basket while the ball is immediately above the goal.
   (p. 94)
56. It is not a violation to strike the ball with the fist.
   (p. 94)
57. The reverse dribble affords better ball protection than the switch dribble.
   (pp. 32–33)
58. When freezing the ball, the center should never handle the ball.
   (p. 77)
59. Basketball was invented as a substitute for the rougher game of football.
   (p. 83)
60. The ten-second rule requires that the ball be passed from one player to another within ten seconds.
   (p. 83)
61. The jump shot is considered the most effective shot in basketball.
   (p. 7)
62. The popularity of the underhand free-throw has declined in recent years.
   (p. 11)
63. The actual floor position of the individual defensive player will vary with the position of the ball.
   (pp. 24–25)
64. Your target for a lay-up shot should be a spot on the backboard twelve to fifteen inches above the goal.
   (p. 4)
65. The ten-second rule has been eliminated for boys' and girls' teams who use the shot clock.
   (pp. 83–84)
66. The three-point shot reduces the number of offensive rebounds.
   (p. 61)
67. Indiana University has built their defense in recent years by forcing the offensive player to drive the baseline.
   (p. 65)

Completion

68. The three basic shots are _____ .
(p. 4)

69. When using the backboard for a lay-up shot, the target should be a spot on the backboard approximately _____ above the goal.
(p. 4)

70. Name some common errors made in shooting the lay-up shot.   (pp. 5–6)

71. The jump shot should be practiced from three situations:

     a. _____

     b. _____

     c. _____
(p. 7)

72. Bunny Leavitt set the world free throw record when he scored _____ consecutive free throws.
(p. 11)

73. What is the secret to good shooting?   (p. 4)

74. What is the major cause of fumbled passes?   (p. 14)

75. Name the four types of passes essential for all players.   (p. 14)

76. The _____ pass is a good one to use in order to pass by a taller opponent or feed a teammate who is in close to the basket.   (p. 16)

77. The _____ pass is necessary during a close exchange of the ball.
(p. 15)

78. Proper pivoting techniques must be mastered in order to avoid _____ violations.
(p. 20)

79. Keeping the body between an opponent and the basket on a rebound attempt is referred to as _____ off the boards.
(p. 21)

80. Individual defensive ability depends on six major factors: _____ .
(p. 22)

81. Proper defensive footwork centers around the _____ step.   (p. 24)

82. The range of the hook shot is no more than _____ feet from the basket.
(p. 30)

83. Coach _____ probably has done more to stimulate interest in the passing-game offense than any other coach.   (p. 53)

84. Defense can be the great _____ .
(p. 63)

85. When a man-for-man defense picks up the opponent at midcourt it is referred to as a _____ defense.   (p. 66)

86. Foremost attention of the zone defense is on the _____ .
(p. 68)

87. The man-for-man defense and zone defense have been combined to result in a _____ defense.   (pp. 73–74)

88. When the opposing team has two unusually high-scoring individuals, a _____ defense may be effective.   (p. 74)

89. _____ time-outs are allowed during a regulation game.   (p. 93)

90. Basketball was invented in _____ at _____ College.
(p. 83)

91. The inventor of basketball was _____ .
(p. 83)

92. The first collegiate game was played in 1897 between _____
    and _____ .
    (p. 83)
93. The most significant single rule change over the years was the elimination of the
    _____ .   (p. 83)
94. The three-second rule was passed in an effort to reduce the effectiveness of the
    _____ .   (p. 84)
95. The free throw lane is _____ feet in width.   (p. 84)
96. The most significant fundamental development in basketball has been
    development of the _____ .   (p. 85)
97. The four most famous basketball teams are _____ .   (p. 86)
98. The basket is _____ feet above the playing floor.   (p. 91)
99. The diameter of the basket is _____ inches.   (p. 91)
100. _____ holds the major-college individual scoring record for a college
    career.   (p. 99)
101. According to one survey, the home team comes out on top _____
    percent of the time in major-college basketball.   (p. 100)
102. Today it is difficult to win unless a team shoots better than _____
    percent.   (p. 100)
103. The shot taken with the shooting arm fully extended is called the _____
    shot.   (pp. 29–30)
104. The rules of the game allow the player holding the ball to step in any direction
    with one foot while keeping the other foot, called the _____
    foot, at its point of contact with the floor.   (p. 20)
105. The University of Tennessee's new arena seats _____ spectators.
    (p. 86)
106. _____ on defense is often the most neglected defensive fundamental.
    (p. 26)
107. The _____ offense is similar to the shuffle in that players learn to
    play all five positions.   (p. 52)
108. The passing game is referred to as the _____ offense.   (p. 53)
109. The distance for the three-point shot is _____ .   (p. 60)
110. The side of the defensive court in which no player has ball possession is called the
    _____ .   (pp. 24–25)

Answers to Evaluation Questions

5   Skill question.
7   A vertical jump on a lay-up shot brings you closer to the basket and provides a
        braking action so your shot strikes the board softly. A vertical jump on the
        jump shot helps prevent falling forward, sideward, or backward with resulting
        decrease in accuracy and possibility of an offensive foul.   (pp. 5,7)
9   Skill question.

12	For both shots the left hand is on the side of the ball and the back of the right hand is facing you, the ball is released from squarely in front by extending the right elbow upward while pushing forward with the forearm and wrist, and the wrist snaps completely forward for a good follow-through. (pp. 7, 11)
14	Good catching technique calls for cupping the hands with fingers spread and thumbs parallel, giving on contact with the ball, watching the ball until it strikes your hands, and concentrating carefully on the act of catching. (pp. 13–14)
16	Skill question.
18	Skill question.
19	Use the control dribble with the left hand to avoid the defensive player. If attacked from both sides, pass or, if possible, evade the opponents. Do not try to dribble between them. (pp. 18–19)
25	Focus on the midsection of the body of the player with the ball, as this part of the body cannot be used in faking. Focus on a point approximately midway between the ball and an opponent without the ball so that you can see both the opponent and the ball by means of peripheral vision. (p. 26)
30	Skill question.
37	Plant the right foot and turn counterclockwise. (p. 33)
49	For a "good" shot, the player must have the skill to make the shot, be unguarded or loosely guarded, and the rebounders must be in position. (p. 46)
51	The shuffle offense is a good choice. It requires more player versatility than the single-pivot offense. (p. 51)
58	The defense might fail if it has been started from the wrong situation, if the initiating player holds the ball too long, or if the players are not skillful enough to handle the ball accurately at such a fast pace. (p. 58)
63	Height, position, speed, and offensive ability. Defensive players should be matched on these qualities to their respective opponents. (p. 65)
64	B should pass the ball to A or C and cut. A should clear to the opposite side of the floor, taking the defensive player out of the play.
68	The opponent is normally picked up just outside the top of the circle, but the pick-up area may range from midcourt to three-quarter to full court. This is also the case in man-for-man defense. (p. 71)
74	The box and one is the better choice because of the greater strength needed in the guard defensive area. (pp. 73–74)
76	Guard tightly if your opponent shoots well from the outside, moves poorly without the ball, is not speedy on the court, or is a poor ball handler. (p. 75)
77	If a freeze is to be attempted, ball handling and free throw ability are most important. (p. 78)
83	The tall-player advantage has been curbed by the three-second rule and the widening of the free throw lane. The rule change making the dunk legal again has restored one tall-player advantage. (p. 84)
89	See definitions. (pp. 89–90)
99	A good percentage of field goals is considered to be better than 40. Bunny Leavitt holds the record for successful consecutive free throws with 499. It has been estimated that the home team wins 80 percent of the time. (pp. 11, 100)

Question Answer Key

Multiple Choice

1. b	5. b
2. c	6. a
3. c	7. c
4. a	

Answer the Following

8. Holding the ball so that the player can shoot, drive, or pass.
9. The speed dribble is used when you must advance the ball quickly downcourt and no defensive players are harassing you. The control dribble is used when defensive players are near and the ball must be protected.
10. To enable the ball-handler to pivot the body between the opponent and the basketball to better protect the ball.
11. Most players now use the push-shot method. This is because the same basic shot which is used in regular play also can be used from the free throw line; as a result the additional practice that would be required to develop the underhand method is not necessary.
12. The ball will float into the air and can be intercepted easily.
13. The speed with which the outlet pass is made after a rebound.
14. a. weak ball-handling team
    b. inexperienced team
    c. poorly conditioned team
    d. methodical-pattern-type team
15. First, you must have ability to shoot the shot. Second, you must not be closely guarded. Third, rebounders must be in position to rebound any missed shot.
16. Relaxation, concentration, and practice.
17. 1986
18. Know how many three-point shooters are on the opposing team, and who they are.
19. Switch on all screens.

True or False

20. F	30. F	40. F	50. F	60. F
21. F	31. F	41. T	51. T	61. T
22. T	32. T	42. T	52. T	62. T
23. T	33. F	43. T	53. F	63. T
24. F	34. F	44. F	54. F	64. T
25. F	35. T	45. T	55. T	65. F
26. F	36. T	46. F	56. F	66. F
27. F	37. T	47. F	57. T	67. T
28. F	38. T	48. F	58. F	
29. T	39. F	49. F	59. F	

Completion

68. lay-up, jump, and free throw
69. twelve to fifteen inches

70. a. jumping off the wrong foot.
    b. laying the ball against the board too hard.
    c. putting spin on the ball.
    d. shooting the ball too low on the backboard.
    e. holding the ball too loosely on takeoff.
    f. failure to concentrate
71. a. from a stationary position
    b. after a dribble
    c. after cutting to receive a pass
72. 499
73. practice
74. not watching the ball all the way into the hands
75. chest, bounce, flip, and two-hand overhead pass
76. bounce
77. flip
78. traveling or walking
79. blocking or screening
80. stance, footwork, position, and vision
81. slide
82. twelve
83. Bob Knight
84. equalizer
85. half-court man-for-man press
86. ball
87. combination
88. triangle and two
89. Five
90. 1891/Springfield
91. Dr. James Naismith
92. Yale/Pennsylvania
93. center jump
94. big player
95. twelve
96. jump shot
97. Original Celtics, Boston Celtics, Los Angeles Lakers and Harlem Globetrotters
98. ten
99. eighteen
100. Pete Maravich
101. 80
102. 40
103. hook
104. pivot
105. 25,000
106. Talk
107. flex
108. motion
109. 19′9″
110. helpside

Index

Alabama, University of, 100
Alcindor, Lew, 85
Army, 99
Astrodome, 86
Auerbach, Arnold, 86

Backboard, 1, 91
Ball-faking, 36–37
Baseball Pass, 30
Basic Types of Shots, 4
Bonus Free-throw Rule, 84
Boston Celtics, 86
Bounce Pass, 15
Box-and-one Defense, 73–74

Carrier Dome, 99
Change-of-pace Dribble, 34
Chest Pass, 15
Chicago, University of, 83
Cincinnati, University of, 99
Combination Defenses, 73–74
Control Dribble, 18
Cornell, 83
Crossover Step, 36

Defense, 22–28
    Desire, 23
    Footwork, 24
    Hints, 27
    Individual, 22–26, 41–42
    Position, 24
    Stance, 23
    Talk, 26
    Vision, 26
Defensive Patterns of Play, 63–74
    Man-for-man, 65–68
    Pressing Defenses, 66–68, 71–72
    Zone Defense, 68–73
Defensive Positioning, 66–67
Defensive Rebounding, 21
Detroit Pistons, 86
Diamond-and-one Defense, 73–74
Double-Post Offense, 48–49

Dribbling, 1, 18, 31–34, 40
    Change-of-pace Dribble, 34
    Control Dribble, 18
    Drills, 34–35
    Hints, 19
    Reverse Dribble, 32–33
    Speed Dribble, 18
    Switch Dribble, 31–32
    When to, 19
Dunking, 85

Fast-break, 57–58
Feet, Care of, 44
Field Goal, 1
Flex Offense, 52
Flip Pass, 15
Floor Balance, 46
Footwork, 24, 63
Foul Shot, 1, 11–12
Four Most Famous Teams, 86
Four Player Zone—One Player Man-for-
    man, 73–74
Free-throw, 1, 11–12
Freeze, When to, 77–78
Full Court Man-for-man Press, 66–68
Furman University, 100

Georgetown, 99
Gymnasium Development, 85–86

Half-court Man-for-man Press, 66–67
Harlem Globetrotters, 86
Hawaii-Hilo, 100
High-Low Offense, 49–50
Holding the Basketball, 3
Home-court Advantage, 100
Hook Pass, 30–31
Hook Shot, 29–30
Houston, Kevin, 99

Illinois, 100
Indiana University, 86, 99
Individual Defense, 22–26
Individual Strategy, 75

Jabbar, Kareem, 85
Johnson, Magic, 86
Jump Shot, 7–11, 85
    Common Errors, 10
    Hints, 7–9

Keys to Passing Game, 54
Kingdome, 86

Lamar University, 99
Lane, Jerome, 99
Language of the Game, 86–90
Lay-up Shot, 4–6
Los Angeles Lakers, 86
Louisiana State University, 99
Louisiana Superdome, 86, 99

Man-for-man Defense, 1, 65–68
    Defensive Positioning, 66–67
    General Principles, 65
    Positioning, 66–67
Maravich, Pete, 99

Naismith, Dr. James, 83
National Association for Intercollegiate
        Athletics, 99
National Basketball Association, 86, 99
National Collegiate Athletic Association, 99
National Junior College Athletic Association,
        99

Offensive Patterns, 47–62
    Double-Post, 48–49
    Flex, 52
    High-Low or 1-3-1, 49–50
    Passing Game, 53–54
    Shuffle, 51
    Single-Post, 47–48
    Zone Offense, 54–57
Offensive Rebounding, 22
One-hand Push Pass, 30
One-on-one Situation, 35–37, 46–47
    Ball Faking, 36–37
    Crossover Step, 36
    Long First Step, 36
One-three-one Half-court Zone Press, 71
One-two-one-one Full Court Zone Press,
        71–72
Original Celtics, 86
Out-of-bounds Situations, 59–60

Passing, 1, 13–17, 30–31, 40
    Baseball Pass, 30
    Bounce Pass, 15
    Chest Pass, 15
    Hook Pass, 30–31
    One-hand Push Pass, 30
    Passing Hints, 16
    Two-hand Overhead Pass, 16
    Types of Passes, 14–16
Passing and Receiving, 13–17
Passing Game, 53–54
Pennsylvania, 83
Peripheral Vision, 26
Physical Condition, 43
Pittsburgh, 99
Pivoting, 20
Playing for One, 76
Pressing Defenses, 66–68, 71–72
Princeton, 99, 100
Pursuit, 72

Rebounding, 2, 20–22, 40–41, 46, 64
    Defensive, 21
    Offensive, 22
Reverse Dribble, 32–33
Riley, Pat, 86
Rules of the Game, 91–95
    Bonus Free-throw Rule, 84
    Forty-five Second Clock, 93
    Ten-second Rule, 83–84
    Thirty-second Clock, 84, 93
    Three-point Shot, 84–85
    Three-second Rule, 84
Rupp Arena, 2, 86

Saperstein, Abe, 86
Selvy, Frank, 100
Shifting, 70
Shooting, 4–13, 29–30, 40
    Basic Types of Shots, 4
    Drills, 12
    Free-throw, 11–12
    Hook Shot, 29–30
    Jump Shot, 7–11
    Lay-up, 4
    Shooting Games, 10–11
Shooting Essentials, 13
Shot Selection, 54
Shuffle Offense, 51
Significant Rule Changes, 83–85
Silverdome, 86
Single-Post Offense, 47–48

Sportsmanship, 97
Springfield College, 83
Stance, 63
Strategy, 75–81
    Individual, 75
    Playing for One, 76
    Team, 75–81
    Use of Time-outs, 78
    When to Press, 76–77
    When to Freeze, 77–78
Strategy for 3-point Shot, 79–81
    Defensive, 80
    Late-Game, 80–81
    Offensive, 79
Switch Dribble, 31–32
Syracuse University, 86

Team Defense, 63–72
    Man-for-man, 65–68
    Pressing Defenses, 66–68, 71–72
    Zone, 68–73
Team Defensive Essentials, 63–64
Team Offense, 45–62
    Double-Post Offense, 48–49
    Flex, 52
    High-Low Offense, 49–50
    Major Essentials, 45–57
    Passing Game, 53–54
    Shuffle, 51
    Single-Post Offense, 47–48
    Zone Offense, 54–57
Technical Foul, 95
Tennessee, University of, 2, 86

Three-Player Zone—Two-Player Man-for-
    Man
Three-Point Shot, 60–62
    Advantages of, 60–61
    Disadvantages of, 61
    Special Three-Point Plays, 62
    Techniques for Getting, 61–62
Three-quarter-court Man-for-man Press,
    66–68
Trap, 72
Triple-threat Position, 3
Two-two-one Full Court Zone Press, 71–72

UCLA, 1, 85

Violations and Penalties, 94–95

Warm-up, 44
Weight Training, 43
Williams, Alan, 99
Wooden, John, 1
Worthy, James, 86

Yale, 83

Zone Defense, 68–73
    Advantages of, 69
    Disadvantages of, 69
    General Principles, 69
    Types of, 70–73
Zone Offense, 54–57
    1-3-1 Attack, 54
    2-1-2 Attack, 54